BASEBALL DAYS

FROM THE SANDLOTS TO "THE SHOW"

Photographs by Henry Horenstein
Essays and Stories by Bill Littlefield

A BULFINCH PRESS BOOK

LITTLE, BROWN AND COMPANY • BOSTON TORONTO LONDON

A Pond Press Book
Designed by Peter A. Andersen

First Edition

Library of Congress Cataloging-in-Publication Data

Horenstein, Henry.
    Baseball days / photographs by Henry Horenstein ; essays by Bill
Littlefield.—1st ed.
        p. cm.
    "A Bulfinch Press Book."
    Includes bibliographical references.
    ISBN 0-8212-1955-3
    1. Baseball.   2. Baseball—Pictorial works.   I. Littlefield,
Bill.   II. Title.
    GV862.5.H67   1993
    769.357—dc20   93-6468

Bulfinch Press is an imprint and trademark of Little, Brown and Company (Inc.)
Published simultaneously in Canada by Little, Brown & Company (Canada) Limited

PRINTED IN SINGAPORE

FOR MARY, AMY, AND ALISON,
THE HEART OF THE ORDER
—*BL*

TO HARRY CALLAHAN,
WHO COACHED ME IN THE MINORS
—*HH*

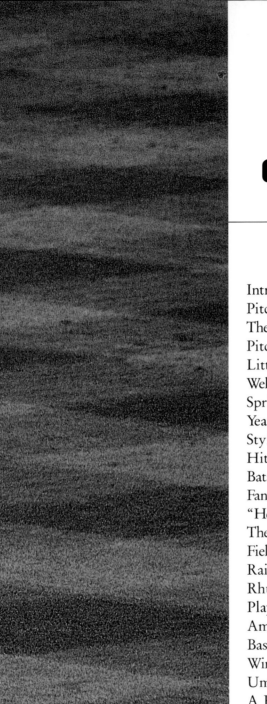

CONTENTS

Introduction   3
Pitchers and Catchers Report   5
The Derivatives   7
Pitching   15
Little League   21
Welcome, Dreamers . . . The Tryout Camp   26
Spring Training   29
Yearning Toward the Show   35
Style   43
Hitting   49
Bats   55
Fans   57
"Hey! Sign This! Sign This! Gimme a Ball!"   65
The Places of the Game   69
Fielding   79
Rain Delay   87
Rhubarbs   89
Players and Their Moments: Johnny Pesky and Luis Tiant   93
Amateur Ball   97
Baseball Man   105
Winter Ball   113
Umpires   121
A Real World Series   129
Old-timers and Their Games   133
Epilogue: Closing Day   143
Acknowledgments   149

BASEBALL DAYS

Duncan Park, home of the Spartanburg Phillies (South Atlantic League), Spartanburg, SC.

INTRODUCTION

BASEBALL DRAWS ATHLETES, of course. Throwing hard or hitting a ball four hundred feet or fielding a grounder that bites the dirt at your toes are all challenges that separate us pretty quickly into the great, the good, the adequate, and the hopeless. Fine athletes are as prized in baseball as in any game, the Mickey Loliches notwithstanding.

Baseball draws fans who like action and drama. Consider the runner and the ball converging at once at the feet of the second baseman, or the perfect peg from right field to catch the astonished runner who has tagged at third and assumed he'll score as a matter of routine. Though there is no clock, the winding down of a pitchers' duel over the course of nine or more innings can be as tense as any sport in which it is time, rather than energy or concentration or luck, that runs out.

But baseball promises more. As many writers have pointed out, the mathematics of the game are at once elegant and mystical. There are so many threes and multiples of three, and Annie Savoy says there are 108 stitches on a baseball and 108 beads in a Catholic rosary. Beyond that, every distance seems to have been established to fairly challenge the players. The great base runner will almost always steal second on the careless pitcher and the average catcher. But it will be close enough so that if the pitching coach can teach the pitcher to pay attention and maybe work a slide step into his delivery, and the catcher can cut down his release time by a fraction of a second, they'll get the runner the next time. Or maybe they'll plant in his runner's head the conviction that he'll need another step away from first, and then they'll pick him off. Then fans who have been paying attention will have a story to tell.

Baseball has history and mythology going for it because it has been played for a long time and people have apparently always felt compelled to write down everything that happened. In 1909, Pryor "Humpy" McElveen had four hits in thirteen pinch-hitting appearances for the Dodgers. As Casey Stengel liked to say, "You could look it up." But looking it up is only the start. Because baseball has changed so little, you can also picture it. Humpy used a smaller glove than the ones the Dodgers have today, but he faced essentially the same challenges today's ballplayers face. His uniform was baggier than today's double knits, but Humpy had the same bad dreams about Christy Mathewson that today's hitters have about Roger Clemens.

Baseball's images are also constant more often than not. You cannot take a picture of anything that isn't before you, but show an old fan a photograph of Dwight Gooden in a batting cage, and the fan will tell you the names and stories of six dead pitchers who could hit.

It is partly the potential for all those stories that attracts writers to baseball, and the presence of time for thinking about the stories helps, too. It is perhaps the tension between the promise of order implicit in the foul lines and the infinite, disorderly possibilities of each pitch that attracts the poets.

Of course before we're old enough to theorize, baseball grabs us for more elemental reasons. Its requirements seem at first deceptively simple. A little kid can throw and catch and even hit a baseball-sized ball long before being able to toss a football in a spiral or heave a basketball up as high as the rim of the basket. A little later, the little kid learns that even the very best baseball players are only normal size.

And, a little later than that, the child goes to a first game. If he or she is lucky, the grass is impossibly green, the home team's uniforms are white, and the sun is shining when the child comes up out of the tunnel and sees the field for the first time—and that child's baseball days have begun.

PITCHERS AND CATCHERS REPORT

The day has dawned to hear again the happiest words in sport . . .
Not "Touchdown!" "Home run!" "Goal!" or "Score!" . . . but "Pitchers
*   and catchers report."*
"Pitchers and catchers report . . ." Such news: concise, flat, stark, and
*   grand.*
It means the game is afoot again, alive once more in the land.
Oh, it'll snow, and cars will stall, and sleet will rattle our nights,
And roundball and hockey will drag us through the play-offs and the
*   fights:*
But somewhere than just in the mind's eye now the motions of baseball
*   start;*
Maybe it's only playing catch, but catch is good for the heart,
And good for the soul, and the arms and the legs, and the head full of
*   off-season talk*
About bar fights and contracts, recalcitrant umpires, and players too
*   eager to squawk*
About vicious injustices, real or imagined, and teams that don't love
*   them enough . . .*
Enough! Time to relish, instead of this filler, returning to all the good
*   stuff.*

In Tucson and Phoenix, in Tampa and Lakeland, they're picking up
*   baseballs for real,*
And tossing them, happily, into their gloves, and secretly thinking,
*   "Some deal,"*
To be gathered again here to stretch in the sun, and scratch, and get
*   loose in the grass,*
To try not to smile in spite of yourself at the best of times coming to
*   pass . . .*

*It won't stop the wars, and it won't fill the bellies of children who've
   lost their relief;*
*It won't house the homeless or patch up the bridges or soften the heart
   of the thief.*
*Still, we can, in this moment and lifetime of trouble, clutch words that
   might offer a sort*
*Of surcease from the madness that hammers us daily; hence, "Pitchers
   and catchers report."*

Pop-up drill. How do you suppose they did this before the invention of the pop-up
machine? *Red Sox spring training, Chain O'Lakes Park, Winter Haven, FL.*

THE DERIVATIVES

WHO KNOWS where it came from?

The English claim that baseball as we know it is descended from a game called rounders, the essentials of which are evident in cricket as well as baseball. Lots of other cultures have their own versions of baseball's beginning. Perhaps the weirdest comes from Russia. Back in the days when the Soviet Union was a union, *Izvestiya* ran an article alleging that baseball was the descendant of a game called *lapta*, which was popular on the steppes when Ivan the Terrible reigned.

Our own grand lie is that baseball sprang full-blown from the mind and heart of Abner Doubleday, a fable so transparently fraudulent that not even the historians who work in the National Baseball Library can recite it without smirking. But no matter. Cooperstown, the bucolic home of the Hall of Fame, Doubleday Field, and a company that still makes wooden bats, would have required inventing if it hadn't already been there. For a game that probably "began" the first time an ape who was neither hungry nor cold tossed a rock into the air and whacked it with a stick just to see if he could do it, Cooperstown is as good a mythical birthplace as any and better than most.

However and wherever it began, baseball has continued to toss off and carry like satellites a variety of other formal and informal games. Some, like the brand of stickball played in the streets of New York over the years, have cultures all their own. On some Manhattan blocks, tales are perhaps still told of how many sewers Willie Mays, who used to play with the kids before or after games at the Polo Grounds, could hit a spaldeen. Stickball requires no field, of course, only a street, a rubber ball, and a broomstick. *Chapitas,* the stripped-down Latin American version of stickball, does without not only the field and the regulation bat, but the ball as well. Kids fish in the storm drains and garbage cans for bottle caps and take turns flipping *them* toward the hitter. To youngsters who graduate from the Chapitas Leagues to an honest baseball field, the ball must look about eight feet across and still as a pie on a windowsill. Maybe it's a good place to

Overleaf: Ted Williams has often said that he thinks hitting a baseball with a bat—whacking a round object with another round object—is the single most difficult act in sports. It's a cinch he never tried to hit a bottle cap with a broomstick. *Caracas, Venezuela.*

start. Roberto Clemente's ballplaying began in the Chapitas Leagues, though the first scout to recruit him for organized baseball did so on the basis of how far the youngster could hit an empty tomato can with a tree branch.

SOFTBALL, another variant, has assumed manifestations more different from each other than from baseball itself. At the low end, clowns and goofs drink beer on the bench and stagger into the trees beyond the outfield to relieve themselves, hoping no one will hit one their way while they're gone. Nobody knows the score. But fast-pitch softball can be quick, competitive, and central to the lives of its adherents. Somewhere between baseball and softball lies the version of the game that an organization in Colorado called the National Fastpitch Association (NFA) is marketing. Convinced that women's pro ball, popular during the late forties and early fifties in the Midwest, can rise again, the NFA has developed a game that features a ball smaller than a regulation softball and a field that is closer to baseball-field size. Stealing is allowed in their game, which is much less pitcher-dominated than fast-pitch softball usually is. If the NFA has its way, by the mid-nineties it will have two divisions (Midwest and Southwest) full of teams at play. At last glance, franchises were for sale at about a million dollars apiece . . . a bargain in these days, when the bidding for men's major league clubs begins at $100 million.

Baseball is packed with legends and lore, but softball doesn't lack for stories worth saving, and its greatest worthies loom over their pastime the way Babe Ruth and Cy Young bestride baseball. Joan Joyce, for years the premier pitcher in the game, won 58 games in a row between August 15, 1959, and July 15, 1962. In her third decade of dominance, she'd hardly slowed down: in 1974 she won 42 games, 13 of which were no-hit, no-run efforts. Kathy Arendsen, Joyce's successor with the mighty Raybestos Brakettes, finished her fifteenth year on the team with a record of 339 wins against 26 losses, but the most stunning statistic in *her* portfolio is her earned run average for 1986. It was 0.00.

Joyce and Arendsen are earnest competitors who have helped lead the Brakettes to twenty-two national championships since 1958, but fast-pitch softball has a showboat and razzmatazz side, too. Late in the summer of 1981, I sat in the concrete bleachers in Frazier Field, the beat-up, old Double-A park in Lynn, Massachusetts, and watched a remarkable pitcher named Rosie Black make fools of a local male all-star team. She was billed as the Queen and Her Court, and the team behind her consisted of a short-stop (her husband), a first baseman (her brother, in drag and a fright wig),

Lisa Fernandez, Raybestos Brakettes. *Textron Lycoming Field, Stratford, CT.*

and a catcher (her sister). Rosie Black struck out eleven men in five innings and gave up only two hits. When she fanned the last three hitters, she was wearing a blindfold. She preceded this impressive performance by announcing from the mound that she wanted to thank God for all the talent he'd given her, but even more for sending us his only son.

Rosie Black was pitching against men that night in Lynn because, as she put it herself, "I can't concentrate on pitching against women, because it's not a challenge. *All* the girls strike out." Joyce and Arendsen have had a similar problem, of course, which partially explains how each was drawn into the dubious exercise of pitching against major league hitters. For the record, Joan Joyce struck out Carl Yastrzemski. Kathy Arendsen K'd Reggie Jackson three times in a row. Each confrontation was the creation of television, where the assumption was that nobody cared how many *women* a great female pitcher could fool or humiliate, but it might be a sexy story if she could tie a man in knots at the plate. Arendsen, for one, has shrugged off the notoriety that resulted from her confrontation with Jackson. "I'm not into this man versus woman thing," she said after the slugger had gone 0-for-3. "I'm into being the best among my peers. But it brought a tremendous amount of publicity to our sport, and we needed and deserved that."

One day, in a more equitable world, women who play team sports brilliantly will get the attention men get for doing the same thing. They will not have to engage in stunts involving male celebrities or wear blindfolds to make the papers. Perhaps sometime the same will be true for some of the men who have chosen to play softball, and there will be TV documentaries about not only Nolan Ryan but also Owen "Fog" Walford, the itinerant New Zealander who could throw a softball more than one hundred miles an hour and pitch five or six nights a week and half a dozen more games over the weekend. Incidentally, though Walford's nickname is as pleasing and perfectly suited to his talents as it can be, it is not the best moniker softball has to offer. A half a century ago in upstate New York, there labored a fellow whose handle rivaled the Big Train, Twilight Ed, Sweet Billy, or any of the other splendid nicknames attached to major leaguers. According to the old guys who still talk about him, he was either laser quick or as slow as a child's last days before Christmas, depending on what the catcher called for. He was Harold "Shifty" Gears.

BEYOND FAST PITCH and slow pitch, other variants of softball are based on all sorts of unlikely qualifications. Whole leagues exist for gay men and others for lesbian women. In St. Petersburg, Florida, there is a

Kids and Kubs is an organization of men over age seventy-five who play a special form of softball. The red base beside the real first base gives the runner and the fielder separate targets so that they won't collide, because if they did, at least 150 years of baseball experience would crash at once. *Northshore Park, St. Petersburg, FL.*

league restricted to very old men. They play in pressed white pants, starched white shirts, and ties. And wherever a handful of blind players can be gathered together, you may find a game called beepball. Predictably, the ball, equipped with an electronic noisemaker, beeps. So do the two bases the game requires. Fielders hear the ball coming and attempt to throw their bodies in front of it. If they get hold of it before the hitter has reached the beeping base, an out is recorded. The scant literature on beepball does not reveal any instance of a fan screaming, "You're deaf!" at an umpire, but it certainly must have happened.

IN 1954, the same year in which Willie Mays made The Catch, historian Jacques Barzun offered this often repeated observation: "Whoever wants to know the heart and mind of America had better learn baseball, the rules and the realities of the game—and do it by watching first some high school or small-town teams." It is perhaps time to update this observation. Whoever wants to know the heart and mind and pain and triumph and ingenuity of the human animal had better check out not only baseball, wherever it turns up, and softball, whether anyone's watching or not, but also stickball, *chapitas,* one-a-cat, wiffle ball, running bases, stoopball, the gay leagues, the old guy leagues, the blind leagues, and the various games of the imagination that a child can play when a rubber ball comes back at him as a grounder or a fly off the garage door or the back steps. It's a mean fact that some children have nothing but bottle caps and balls of rolled-up paper to throw at one another, a fact that should engender in us shame and the determination to make a better world. But we can also smile at the games children make of nearly nothing; we can see hope in that capacity. And we can celebrate, as we consider all the manifestations of baseball, the undeniable spirit of affirmation present in the desire and the determination of so many to play merely for the joy that our best game offers.

PITCHING

THE GAME BEGINS with pitching.

This is, of course, literally true. Lefty Grove, who won three hundred games and ended up in the Hall of Fame, knew that. In a game against the Yankees one day, Jimmy Foxx took Grove into the third deck. The next time Foxx came to the plate, Grove just stood on the mound and watched him. When his catcher finally trotted out to see what was wrong, Grove said, "Let's just wait a minute more. Maybe he'll get a long-distance phone call." And Grove was not the only pitcher to adopt that defensive strategy. Most of the fellows who pitched for Casey Stengel's Mets subscribed to it. On one representative day, the Professor had made one of his many trips to the mound to relieve his starting pitcher. He'd signaled the bullpen several times for the reliever he wanted, but the door to the bullpen remained closed. Finally, the plate umpire came out to ask Stengel to explain the delay.

"I dunno," said Casey, whose Mets set a modern-day record by losing 120 games in 1962, "I guess they're all afraid to come out."

Perhaps the greatest surprise is that more pitchers everywhere haven't been afraid to assume the position. Pitchers would be sitting ducks if they were allowed the relative security of sitting. Instead, all but the most acrobatic of them are falling one way or another, off to the left or the right, but always *toward* the guys who can slam the ball back at them, which is a grisly thought. Ask Herb Score, who took a line drive in the face and was never the same pitcher afterward. Or Dizzy Dean, who got hit on the *toe* by a batted ball and never again recovered his natural motion.

So any consideration of pitching should probably begin with the recognition that nobody in his right mind voluntarily stands that close to a man who can redirect a baseball at his head or his groin so quickly that his chance to protect himself would be virtually nil.

Nolan Ryan, God's little joke on every other forty-something man on the planet, recognized that truth years ago, but he is the sort of baseball genius who has made it work *for* him. "It helps if the hitters think you're a little crazy," he once said. That was in the days before Ryan became the aggressively uncrazy owner of a bank. He was merely the possessor of a fastball that topped out at about one hundred miles an hour and a fellow who cheerfully admitted that on some days he had no particular idea where it might go. Through the middle years of his nearly unprecedented career, Ryan regularly led the major leagues in both walks *and* strikeouts. His wild pitches were sometimes serious . . . head-high, hissing reminders that there are lots of other ways to make a living besides hitting.

See what has happened here? This is an essay written by a hitter. Look how quickly it has slipped the track of considering the perils a pitcher faces and made straight for the writer's own gut knowledge of the *bottom* truth: pitchers are superhuman and dangerous.

This is not to suggest that they do not have problems. Consider, as everyone who has ever tried to make sense of pitching has done, Steve Blass. From 1964 through 1972, he pitched admirably for the Pittsburgh Pirates. Then, suddenly, he couldn't do what he'd always been able to do. His control deserted him, and nobody could figure out why. He had been a pitcher, and suddenly he wasn't anymore. That flat fact became hideously and forever evident during a game Blass tried to pitch against Atlanta early in the '73 season. Over the course of one and a third innings, Steve Blass gave up seven runs on five hits, six walks, and three wild pitches. Recalling that day for Roger Angell two years later, Blass said, "It was the worst experience of my life. I don't think I'll ever forget it. I was embarrassed and disgusted. I was totally unnerved. You can't imagine the feeling that you suddenly have no *idea* what you're doing out there, performing that way as a major league pitcher. It was kind of scary."

This is the sort of horror over which people discussing pitching shake their heads, but the astonishing thing is that it does not happen more often. Baseball is a game characterized by the isolation of all the players. A short-stop who boots a ground ball can't blame the second baseman for not blocking for him. But the player who is most alone is the pitcher. And he is also the most dramatic center of attention in all of sports. As he swings into his motion and gets ready to deliver the ball, the only people in the ballpark who aren't watching him are those buying or selling hot dogs or beer. The sort of person who wants to pitch is the same sort of person who wants to be president, but presidents remain in demand for interviews for years after they've demonstrated that they can't do the job. If they are lucky, pitchers get to go to the far end of the bullpen bench when that happens. There, they try to look inconspicuous as they wonder what went wrong.

Of course, when all is well with a pitcher, the result is splendid to behold for everyone but the hitter. The great and successful pitcher is physically graceful to the point of dance, wise enough to understand and just barely avoid from moment to moment the boundary between the frontier of his own ability and the batter's talent and nerve, and mean as hell's weather. Or maybe he can just bring heat.

Perhaps the most fascinating thing about pitching is that you can succeed at it by so many different means. It's fine to be able to throw a high, hard one at ninety miles an hour, but a slow curve when the batter is looking for the fastball will be just as effective. Control would seem to be essential, but pitchers famous for their lack of same have also prospered for years. Ryne Duren, who lasted for eleven seasons in the big leagues, used to regularly throw a warm-up pitch up on the screen just to remind batters that

Cal Eldred is the rare rookie pitcher who got it right early . . . and even he looks impossibly unnatural committing this most unnatural of acts. *Oriole Park at Camden Yards, Baltimore, MD.*

on some occasions he had no control at all; and lots of knuckleballers only launch the ball in the general direction of the plate and hope for the best. Serious discipline should be required of fellows for whom the difference between a great pitch and a gopher ball may be less than an inch one way or another, but as a group, pitchers are without question less disciplined than their teammates.

The art of pitching is not without its focused and solemn disciples. Tom Seaver and Steve Carlton come to mind. But Grover Cleveland Alexander, Rube Waddell, and many of the other great baseball drinkers have been pitchers, and if you ask most fans for a list of the game's flakes, they'll come up with Dizzy Dean, Bo Belinsky, Sparky Lyle, and several dozen other pitchers before they mention a third baseman or a catcher. (For the record, Dean's evaluation of the game's pitchers began with, "I don't recall seeing any better than myself"; Belinsky once said, "My only regret in life is that I can't sit in the stands and watch me pitch"; Sparky Lyle liked to get naked in the locker room and jump, tail first, into his teammates' birthday cakes.)

The lopsided presence of so many drinkers, large talkers, and cake jumpers on the mound may be partially explained by the fact that pitching is an unnatural act. Children learn that early. All good Little League coaches tell their pitchers not to throw curveballs. The explanation for this advice is that the repetitive jerk of the wrist and elbow that the pitch requires will damage young tissue and joints. While this is true, it's only part of the story. With the exception of knuckleballers, who are really base-ball *pushers* rather than pitchers, everybody who throws overhand hard and a lot is beating up his arm, curveball or no curveball. That's why the pitcher being interviewed after the game has a bulging bag of ice strapped to his elbow, or his shoulder, or both if he has a clever and dexterous trainer.

Which brings up one of the great mysteries of pitching: why don't pitchers who play baseball imitate their counterparts on the softball field? Great softball pitchers can make the ball do more than even the greatest baseball pitchers can. (There is no "riser" in baseball, but in softball, that is the pitch that sends many would-be hitters over to the tennis court.) Pitching underhanded is a natural motion that does no particular damage to the arm, the proof of which is that men and women who pitch softball can work in several games a day, which would be preposterous for baseball pitchers. Softball pitchers are certainly no slower than their baseball counterparts. In each case, the most accomplished hurlers can bring the ball at nearly one hundred miles an hour. So why do baseball's pitchers continue to sub-scribe almost exclusively to the overhand motion that annually burns out prospects from Little League on up and requires the pros to undergo ten-don transplants in the off-season?

Hitting is timing. Pitching is upsetting timing. This pitcher, like any good one, has about eleven different ways to foul up your swing. Long may she bring heat. *Belles vs. Brakettes, Smith Field, Parsippany, NJ.*

Boston Park League, Casey Field, Dorchester, MA.

Maybe it's part history, part habit, part myth . . . though all the illustrations I've ever seen show David firing sidearm at Goliath. Maybe it's also part macho pride. Coming hard and overhand in our culture is more direct, less sneaky, less wimpy than dropping down. Constantly *risking* a torn rotator cuff is part of the deal, I suppose, and why they're paid the big bucks.

That all sounds pretty tentative, but no wonder. Though it is perhaps possible to understand a few of the component parts of the art of pitching at once, together they resist us and pull against each other. As a great pitcher, Jim Palmer, once said of a great manager, Earl Weaver, "The only thing he understands about pitching is that he couldn't hit it." In that respect, at least, the old Earl of Baltimore has a great deal of company.

LITTLE LEAGUE

HAY FEVER is a problem for some Little Leaguers. I don't know what the big leaguers who are allergic to spring do about it, but Little Leaguers generally sniffle, snort, rub their red eyes, and wipe their noses on the sleeves of their uniforms. That is what I did until my parents got tired of hearing me complain. Then they got the pediatrician to give me an antihistamine. I took it. I was thirteen. What did I know about mixing drugs with baseball?

Sometime in the early innings of a game played on a very hot day, the antihistamine kicked in. My reflexes, which were never especially good, lagged. I was a catcher. If I'd been a right fielder, probably nobody would ever have known the difference, but you can't hide a catcher. The pitcher was the coach's son. He was one of those boys who was shaving in sixth grade. One summer day a year or so later, I was riding the bus home from my job as a day-camp counselor . . . a good job for a junior high school kid. This guy who had been the pitcher that day got on the bus a stop after I did. His muscles bulged out of his T-shirt, which was covered with dirt and tar. He had a summer job as a roofer. He had a six-pack of beer in his hand. I think he went right from junior high school to the University of Michigan, where he starred as a blocking back for some years.

Anyway, this man among boys who was the pitcher fired a third strike past a frightened hitter on this very hot afternoon, and though I was behind the plate, more or less in position to catch the ball, I didn't. It kicked off my glove and rolled out along the dusty first baseline. The batter, filled with the adrenaline that fear of death by fastball will bring, raced toward first base like a man reprieved. Addled by the antihistamine, I hunted wearily for the ball, found it, picked it up, and then threw it far enough to the first baseman's left to pull him off the bag.

"Goddamnit!" shouted the coach. He slammed down his score book and came at me like a truck. He was beefy, and he had a flattop. If I'd been quicker, I'd have run from him. He grabbed the strap that held my chest protector on and hissed at me. "Take that equipment off. That was a strike-

The late Carl Stotz invented Little League, probably because he wanted to manage.
Carl E. Stotz Field, Williamsport, PA.

Opposite: If this guy has just kicked a field goal, his form is flawless. Otherwise, who knows what he's up to? *Yellowjackets Field, Tampa, FL.*

out you loused up. You're out of the game." He looked up and beckoned to the boy playing center field; he was the one who would take my place as catcher.

I remember that there were trees overhanging our bench. It was shady there. It was less hot. I remember the lacy patterns the sun made where it came through the leaves, so while I was sitting on the bench, I must have been looking at the ground, or at my feet. I think I remember wondering if it would be okay for somebody who'd been yanked out of the game and publicly humiliated to get a drink of water from the fountain.

Little League isn't always that bad. Sometimes it is neither cruel nor perverse. Sometimes it is just goofy. For every stereotypical Little League mother or father who roars stupidly at an umpire or makes her or his kid walk home after striking out, half a dozen youngsters are standing happily in the outfield weeds somewhere with baseball gloves on their heads.

One happy truth about Little League is that lots of girls play now. Like Major League Baseball five decades ago, Little League had to be dragged into the age of equal opportunity by a few tenacious individuals, but for the most part, gender is no longer the barrier it used to be for preadolescent ballplayers. I say for the most part because of a story told to me in 1989 by a mother who called the commissioner of the Little League in which her daughter played in order to suggest that the relatively few girls in the league should not be isolated, one to a team.

"Lady," the commissioner replied, "it's a little boys' game."

That this exchange occurred in the People's Republic of Cambridge, Massachusetts, suggests that even in areas of high consciousness, a retrograde sexism persists, despite the best efforts of pioneer infielders with names like Melissa and Jane, not to mention their determined parents and the courts.

But we shouldn't blame that on Little League, and maybe even letting such solemn issues as gender and politics creep into the discussion is dumb. When we let the kids play, Little League is about the day the tiny child who can only almost manage the team's lightest bat and always gets tucked away in right field lucks out. Late in a game that already stands at about 22–16 against, he or she peers into a cloudless blue sky to find the ball coming hard, like fate and danger. In a clumsy, desperate motion, the glove comes up. Probably the eyelids come down. Miraculously, the ball lands where it is supposed to land. It does not bounce away. It does not rip the glove from the astonished fielder's hand. There is a moment of silence, and then a shout of one part triumph and two parts raucous disbelief. "Did you see that! Oh, my God!"

Rounding second base, the suddenly irrelevant runner looks out into

right field, turns toward his teammates on the bench, then looks out there again. "How the heck—?" he thinks. He kicks the dirt, DiMaggio-style, feeling as cheated as the Clipper himself did when Al Gionfriddo caught the ball that seemed as if it would surely win the World Series for the Yankees in 1947. For a moment about as durable as a soap bubble, the children are one with their major league counterparts. In another minute, the subs behind each bench will be tickling each other with twigs to pass the time that this eternal game is taking. But at the right fielder's dinner table tonight, there will be telling and retelling . . . celebration and ice cream.

Yellowjackets Field, Tampa, FL.

WELCOME, DREAMERS...
THE TRYOUT CAMP

GEORGE DIGBY, a longtime scout, was asked a few years ago how he could distinguish the bona fide prospects from the also-rans among the thousands of young men he scouted each year.

"Well," Digby said, "an old scout said to me when I was first starting out, 'Don't ever force yourself to like somebody. Let him make you quiver. If he don't make you quiver, he's not any good.'"

There are, in addition to the many impostors at the tryout camps, those who make the scouts quiver, but they are rarely surprises. The best players are the ones who've been invited to attend the camps by the Major League Bureau scouts because they've already seen those fellows play, and they know the scouts from the individual teams will want to see them, too. These are the boys who arrive in full uniform and already know the routine. They are patient with the business of filling out the Scouting Bureau cards. When their numbers are called, they run sixty yards in seven seconds or less. The outfielders among this elite group hop once in the grass and throw peas and pills that skid on one bounce into the glove of the catcher. The pitchers warm up slowly and then fire low fastballs out of the same motion, over and over again, until the man behind them quietly says, "Now break one off." Then they throw curveballs that dip and disappear under the catcher's thigh.

But such composure is only for the veterans of the tryout camps, the fellows who know they are good enough to be signed. For the hundred or more boys at every camp who don't fall into that category, the day is full of miserable surprises. The first thing they learn is that they'll spend most of their time standing around waiting, which is actually pretty good preparation for the big leagues. As former pitcher Bill Lee once said, "In baseball, you're supposed to sit on your ass, spit tobacco, and nod at stupid things." But next they find that if they *can't* run sixty yards in about seven seconds and hit a catcher 260 feet away on one bounce, nobody's going to care much what they *can* do. After several hours of timed heats and throwing drills, only twenty or so of the quickest kids with the strongest arms get to play in a simulated game. And only the fortunate and glorious few picked to play in the game get to swing a bat even once. It's a deal rigged to break the heart of a great hitter who's *only* a great hitter. Once, I overheard a veteran scout talking to a husky college outfielder who was disconsolate at not having been picked to play in the simulated game.

"Son," said the scout, "you must be a hell of a hitter."

The boy looked at the old man and hope leapt into his eyes. "I am," he said. "But how'd you know that?"

"Well," the scout said, "you got a uniform on, so you made a team somewhere, and you can't run or throw."

At another camp, I watched the pitchers labor, one after another, as the scouts, sitting behind them in lawn chairs, glanced from the boys to the speed guns that were mercilessly timing each throw. Behind the scouts stood the fellows who were waiting for a turn to show their stuff. As a group, they'd been told before the drill started that while they didn't have to throw ninety-five miles an hour, like Lee Smith or Roger Clemens, they'd better be in the middle eighties with their fastballs. Now, they watched in dismay as the gun caught some of the fastest pitches they'd ever seen at seventy-two . . . seventy-five . . . seventy-three . . . seventy-three . . .

When it came time for the pitcher working in front of them to throw his curve, he broke off an impressive hook. Or at least the little boys leaning against their bicycles behind the catcher were impressed.

"Did you see that?" one piped.

"How'd he do that?" said the other, a soprano like his pal.

The pitcher allowed himself a smile, but Tom Bourque, the scout running that part of the camp, wasn't fooled. "Fellas," he said to the youngsters on the bikes, "that's why you'll be playing lacrosse in a couple years. Next."

"Do they tell you right away if you make it?" wondered the boy who'd pointed out that there was no mound. He won the day's award for lunatic optimism.

STILL, that pitcher has some slim grounds for hope. He does look like a ballplayer. He's dressed in the uniform of his high school team. When it's his turn, he will demonstrate that he can throw strikes.

But at the same camp there is a heavy fellow in chino pants and an extralarge Celtics T-shirt . . . the kind with a colorful picture of the team on the front. He wears black, high-top sneakers instead of spikes. He is allegedly an outfielder, but while the other candidates run their sixty yards in just over seven seconds, he runs his in just under eighteen. When he throws from the outfield, the catcher has to jog almost to second base to collect the balls. Yet, nobody tells him to go home. He gets three throws, just like everybody else. While he watches the others, he pounds his fist into his glove, intense and jumpy. He is a little bug-eyed, but nobody laughs. On its best days, baseball has room for everybody. And, of course, for those with no chance, the satisfaction of having tried still remains, as well as the consolation of the stories that time will encourage. In a few years, everyone who was present, even the guy in the Celtics shirt, will be able to say, "I ran and threw for the scouts, just like Jeff Reardon and Tom Glavine . . . just like Jackie Robinson and Willie Mays." And the years will shrink the distance between those who were chosen and those who were not, until the storytellers will begin to believe that if they hadn't been tired that morning, or if the grass hadn't been a little slick, they might have made a little better impression, might have been asked to play in the simulated game, might have had a chance to hit . . . and that might have made all the difference.

Scouts, Major League Tryout Camp. *Palmer Field, Middletown, CT.*

SPRING

TRAINING

ONCE UPON A TIME, spring training made sense. Thirty and forty and fifty years ago, when ballplayers could be counted on to get fat over the winter, it was a necessity. Think of Babe Ruth in a rubber suit, an old heavyweight laboring around the perimeter of the outfield as the Florida sun melted the beer and ice cream off his frame. And think of the newsreel cameras there to record the Babe's clowning as well as his work. Before television, the scratchy, jumpy black-and-white film gave fans back home in New York and Boston and Detroit the promise that baseball was under way again to the south and that it would soon be with them once more at the ballpark, a bus or subway ride away.

In those days, spring training made simple business sense, too. A series of Florida land booms had created towns out of wilderness and swamp. When baseball arrived, even if only for five weeks a year, it was good for everybody. The players got dependable weather for their running and throwing. The residents got some entertainment where there hadn't been much of it. The owners got the gate.

The model for the early sites was Vero Beach, spring home of the Dodgers. The club picked up a defunct military base for peanuts and piled every player employed by the organization into the barracks there. It wasn't pretty, but it worked. In Vero Beach, aka Dodgertown, no veteran could relax, because if he did and General Manager Branch Rickey caught him, Rickey would point out a kid two diamonds over who was hungry for a major league job. Rickey is sometimes celebrated as Saint Branch, the man who integrated the major leagues by employing the carefully chosen Jackie Robinson in 1947. But lots of players also knew him as a canny and ruthless negotiator and a fellow who could fish a dollar out of a fan's pocket and leave him smiling every time.

Many of the subsequent spring training camps were built on the Dodger blueprint, though few of them managed to create the Disneyesque attraction that Dodgertown eventually became. In Vero now, the paths and streets that lead from the cafeteria to the ball fields are named after old

Writers sent to cover spring training insist they are working. Players do, too. *Red Sox spring training, Chain O'Lakes Park, Winter Haven, FL.*

Opposite above: Roger McDowell and son, ballplayers. *Dodgertown, Vero Beach, FL.*
Opposite below: "I don't love you because you're Italian. I love you because *I'm* Italian."
Tommy Lasorda, Dodgertown, Vero Beach, FL.

Dodgers, and everything is painted Dodger Blue. Games are sold out well in advance. Hollywood stars have been known to turn up in the clubhouse or behind the dugout. How can the Expos or the Rangers compete with that?

THE SPRING TRAINING of the old newsreels was simple, and its attractions were obvious. It was fun to see the sluggers limber up against a background of palm trees, and if you could make it to Florida yourself, you stood a fair chance of shaking the hand of one of the heroes. Security was lax, and nobody was in a hurry. Everybody did a lot of sitting around. If you couldn't walk up to the ticket booth and buy a seat at game time, it was only because the guy who was supposed to be selling the tickets had fallen asleep in the sun somewhere.

But over the last decade or so, spring training has become a big and sometimes ugly business. Popular teams such as the Cubs and the Red Sox sell out their exhibition games weeks and even months in advance, leaving lines of disappointed boys and their addled grandfathers gaping in the parking lot each afternoon. Scalpers abound. Once-small Florida towns engage in vigorous competition for spring training franchises, each hoping to reinvent itself by identifying with a ball club for a while until some other town offers the team a better deal. The Grapefruit League ballparks were once invariably cozy throwbacks . . . clattery wooden places with outfield fences full of advertisements for the drugstore, the dry cleaner, and the local paper. Now, teams such as Kansas City and Texas have built spiffy new parks with dimensions identical to the stadia back home . . . clean, well-lighted places without funk or mystery.

The ethics of the regular season have also trickled down to Florida to a discouraging extent. Several years ago, in Lakeland, where the Tigers train, I saw Kirk Gibson snatch a tape recorder away from a writer because he thought the writer was trying to electronically eavesdrop on Gibson and his teammates. Obviously in midseason form, Gibson swore at the writer and threatened to shatter the tape recorder for laughs. A year later, in Tampa, then the March home of the Reds, I left the half-empty press box with a blind fan who'd been kicked out by the team's public relations director. The fan had traveled from Cincinnati to be in the presence of his team for a while, but that meant nothing to this fellow with proper press credentials on his small, gray, button-down mind. It's not, of course, that these stories don't belong in the big leagues. But there was a time when anybody cranked up for violence or gratuitous cruelty at spring training would have been considered out of step.

This is not to suggest that the phenomenon of Florida baseball in the spring doesn't retain some of its charms. The Mets, humorless and paranoid, may restrict interviews with their stars, and security guards may patrol most of the foul lines. But among the stars themselves there are always one or two in Florida who have not yet grown grumpy or "focused" enough to ignore their admirers, and the guards are older, less well-armed, and more inclined to say the hell with it when kids try to sneak past them in search of autographs.

Beyond that, there is the sense of fun that comes from the fact that, during spring training, nothing counts yet. Managers who have more pitchers than they know what to do with will sometimes agree to continue beyond nine innings in a game that isn't tied, just to give the extra guys some work. Players who've left the lineup will jog around in the outfield and trade quips with their opponents while the game is still going on. Around the pool at the Holiday Inn, as the day is coming to a close, relief pitchers will play tag with their children while you watch, reminding you that they are not heroes, or not only heroes, but also men young for this short time and blessed to be in a business most of us think of as play.

Once, when the large and still fearsome Dave Parker was near the end of his career, I watched him take batting practice in the red dirt of a field in Tampa after almost everyone else had gone home. As each fat fastball came in, Parker would address it. "I'm sorry, baby," he would say in a strangely high-pitched voice, "but I got to do it." Whack! The ball would disappear in a long curve over the bright green outfield wall. "I love you." Whack! "But you got to go now." Maybe it was the same during batting practice in Cincinnati that season, but I like to think not.

Prospects in the Philadelphia Phillies organization. Sometimes, late in the season, the big club invites some of its most promising minor leaguers to see a game in the big club's park. Everybody tries not to laugh at their ties. *Veterans Stadium, Philadelphia, PA.*

YEARNING TOWARD
THE SHOW

IF BASEBALL in the big leagues is chartered jets, minor league baseball is bus rides. Every man who has ever ascended the narrow ladder to a manager's job in the majors has a story about the day in the minors when the bus driver got so drunk that the manager had to transport the El Paso Diablos, the Quad City River Bandits, or the Myrtle Beach Hurricanes by himself. Either that or the bus broke down and everybody had to walk—and then play a doubleheader.

Meal money in A Ball, the first step up toward the show after Rookie League, is about eleven dollars a day. At AAA, where the distance between you and the show might be no more than a major leaguer's sprained ankle or cranky back, you get about fourteen dollars. Small wonder that lots of fellows who finally make it to the big leagues and the big contracts say their toughest adjustment is not learning how to hit better pitching; it's figuring out how to spend the fifty or sixty dollars a day they're suddenly getting for food when they've been eating exclusively at McDonald's for the past six or eight years.

Nor is it just a matter of waiting confidently for the days of wine and sirloin to arrive. Of all the young men who sign contracts to play baseball professionally, only about 7 percent ever pull on a big league jersey. That means that 93 percent of all those boys who have been the best player their high school ever produced will play pro ball only in places such as Albany, Pawtucket, Lethbridge, and Old Orchard Beach. When it turns cold, they'll look for chances to hook on with teams in Jalisco, Tabasco, or Aragua. When they admit to themselves that the string is running out on this side of the ocean, they'll think about baseball in Japan, Australia, Italy, or Holland. They'll investigate rumors that a peculiar and growing interest in the game among the French may lead to something there.

Some minor leaguers stall in the bushes because they simply don't turn out to be as fast or as strong or as durable as the scouts who signed them hoped they would be. Some eat or drink their way out of baseball. Some find they cannot sustain their commitment to a game that may or may not

Overleaf: One day each of these kids will impress a wide-eyed child by telling him or her what it was like to sign a pro contract and play "away ball." It will be a big deal. *Legion Park, home of the Great Falls Dodgers (Pioneer League), Great Falls, MT.*

From late February until early April, the minor leaguers train with the millionaires in Florida and Arizona. But when the bell rings and the big leaguers head for Atlanta, San Francisco, and Montreal, the kids all go to Calfee Park. *Calfee Park, Pulaski, VA.*

ever reward them and that requires of them a routine that will bore many of them stupid before they ever have an opportunity to make any money at it. In the minor leagues, as in the majors, most games are at night. Even the most dedicated competitor can work out and psyche himself up for the game for only a few hours a day. How do you kill the rest of the time in Bluefield, West Virginia, when it's still six hours to batting practice? Take a nap? Rerent the same videos you've already seen eleven times? Pat Jordan, who wrote about his days of unfulfilled promise in the Braves' minor league system in a wonderful book called *False Spring*, remembers that mostly he shopped for Ban-lon shirts in every available color. That's okay if you can make the clerk in the clothing store understand you when you say "Ban-lon," but what if you're from the Dominican Republic, seventeen years old, away from home for the first time, and armed only with phrases such as, "A hamburger and fries, please," and "Go piss up a rope"? Your manager doesn't speak Spanish, and neither do most of your teammates. You've never read a whole book. The junior high school kids goosing each other in the stands remind you of how much you miss your friends. And even on the nights when you go 2-for-4 with an RBI and throw a couple of guys out from deep in the shortstop hole, nobody seems to notice. Some suck it up and keep dreaming. Some mope around for a while and then go home. Others get angry and turn that anger to determination and then get called Latin hotheads for the rest of their baseball days, whether those days take them to the big leagues or not.

It is not easy for the owners, either, because in the peculiar economy of baseball, the minor league owner really doesn't own much of anything. The big league club sends him the players, who don't want to be there any longer than they have to be and who are likely to be snatched away when they demonstrate that they're any good. This and desperation go some distance toward explaining the goofy string of promotions that you will encounter at almost all minor league ballparks. On one night a guy in a fright wig and a baseball suit will juggle and dance at second base. On another, a woman known as the Dynamite Lady will climb into a cardboard box about three feet square and blow herself up. Max Patkin, the self-styled Clown Prince of Baseball, once had a particularly spectacular routine, in which he would fire a baseball skyward from a cannon-style pitching machine that he had mounted in the back of a jeep. Then he would gun the jeep into center field, where he would catch the ball. The groundkeepers must have been amused.

In the Double-A park in Reading, there used to be air shows before the game and a chance to sign up with the Air Force Reserve at home plate if you were sufficiently moved by the spectacle. At Stumpf's Field in

Lancaster, Pennsylvania, there were sometimes pro wrestling matches between games of doubleheaders, but Stumpf's lies fallow now, and the practice has not caught on elsewhere. And then there was the promotion that none of the members of the 1965 High Point-Thomasville Hi-Toms of the late and much lamented A-Ball Western Carolina League will ever forget. It seems that one night, Miss North Carolina, Sharon Finch, was induced to throw out the first ball at a Hi-Toms game. She handled the task adequately, but made the mistake of staying around to see the mayor of Thomasville throw out a first pitch of his own. The mayor let go a high hard one and clipped Miss North Carolina on the jaw, knocking her both unconscious and into the grasp of astonished Hi-Tom manager Ralph Rowe. Rowe did his best to maintain dignity and composure while the young beauty queen sprawled, moaning, in his arms, but his players were no help at all. They whistled and shrieked for their manager to put the moves on Miss North Carolina while he had the chance. Some say that Rowe never regained control of that particular edition of the Hi-Toms.

Behind the spectacular and semispectacular stunts is the constant effort to keep the customers coming back, whether the team is any good or not. Minor league baseball is the adman on the run, Willie Loman in his rookie year. That's why, in every minor league park, night after night, if you turn to page twelve in your program and match the number in the upper right-hand corner with the one the announcer is about to read, you can win anything from an ice cream cone at the Dairy Queen after the game to a free car wash at Barry's Super Clean or six bucks worth of dry cleaning at Sal's. The advertising on the outfield wall is sometimes a hoot, too. At the big league parks, it's all Winston and Bud Lite. But in right center field at RiverSide Stadium on City Island Park, in the middle of the Susquehanna River, home of the Harrisburg Senators, a shining gold-on-royal-blue billboard reads: The Best Lawyers in America—Angino and Romer.

It is heartening that over the last decade or so, minor league baseball has made a comeback. Dreamers have suggested that this means the public has tired of the steady diet of televised games. They've celebrated the return of people to firsthand experience as evidence that the population at large may not be as couch-bound and brain-dead as it once seemed to be. That may be a reach, but the relative health of minor league operations in minor league towns does somehow suggest that folks have discovered again the basic attractions of a game that does not require electronic analysis by former pros, a domed home, or even a computerized scoreboard capable of reproducing every play. If you're paying attention the first time, you don't have to see it again. You get a better seat in the minors, and you get it for less. The players will look as big and strong and talented to your kids as

Foul ball. Hold the sunset, and we'll do it again. *Grainger Stadium, home of the Kinston Indians (Carolina League), Kinston, NC.*

"Do it my way. And stand up straight!" *Hub Kittle, Roving Pitching Instructor, St. Louis Cardinals, Howard Johnson Field, home of the Johnson City Cardinals (Appalachian League), Johnson City, TN.*

the major leaguers would look, and most of the minor leaguers will stick around to sign autographs as long as there's anyone left to ask. If the car they're giving away between innings is an '82 Suburu rather than a shiny, new Blazer, so what? The peanuts are fresh, and the beer is cold, and you probably won't win anyway. Go, you Mudhens.

STYLE

THE BATTER PICKS UP a sledgehammer, the head of which has been wrapped with about sixty yards of athletic tape against the possibility that it might fly off into the stands in a really macabre accident. He swings it gingerly, without real enthusiasm. He is in a slump, and he can't overlook any help that might be available. Someone in the dugout has sworn by the sledgehammer.

Next the batter moves to the on-deck circle, where he picks up a rag covered with pine tar and rubs the handle of his bat with it. The handle is already black with tar, but he rubs it again, three swipes and a half turn at the knob of the bat when he's finished. Then he transfers a little of the pine tar to his hands and dusts them with rosin from the bag in the circle. He adjusts the wristbands on both wrists.

When it is his turn to approach the plate, the hitter covers the few yards with purpose, or so it appears. Don't be fooled. As soon as he can get the umpire's attention, he calls time-out. He takes two level practice swings. He adjusts his batting helmet. He taps the sole of each foot twice with the barrel of the bat to knock the dirt from his spikes, though there is no dirt in his spikes. This effort has disturbed the batting helmet, which the hitter now adjusts again and then mashes onto his head with the heel of his hand. With the toe of his right foot, he digs at a little hole deep in the batter's box. It must feel right, this hole, and its doesn't yet. The batter digs and pivots some more. When he has the hole right, he nods to the umpire that he is ready. He takes the knob of his bat in the tips of the fingers of his left hand and lets it swing once like a pendulum across the inside part of the plate. Then he puts his right hand back on the bat and half swings it, making sure that the outside part of the plate is also within reach, although it is utterly impossible that he does not know it is.

The batter has time to take these measurements, even after he has stepped back into the box, because the pitcher has wandered off the rubber to look for *his* rosin bag. He finds it behind the mound and

Rob Dibble, Cincinnati Reds. If a batter hits the pitch Dibble has just thrown back at him, maybe Dibble will knock it down with his nose; his glove will be somewhere out around second base. *Candlestick Park, San Francisco, CA.*

Opposite: Jose Rijo of the Reds will sometimes throw a ball ninety miles an hour under a batter's chin. But first he has to get the dirt right. *Candlestick Park, San Francisco, CA.*

tosses it gently into the air, bounces it lightly off his palm twice and then once off the back of his hand, although no pitcher has ever thrown a ball out of the back of his hand. He adjusts his cap, wipes his hand across his brow to plant in the batter's mind the possibility that the next pitch might be wet, rosin notwithstanding. He digs with the toe of *his* right foot at the little hole in front of the pitching rubber. It is nearly as resistant to perfection as the hole in the batter's box. He adjusts his cap again and looks in toward the catcher for his sign. Everywhere in the park the expectation grows that soon he will throw a pitch . . . except that now the batter has called time again. He steps out of the box to tug at his pants. He puts the heel of his hand on the top of his helmet again and jams it even more tightly onto his head. What can have caused it to come loose? He hasn't swung. He hasn't done anything . . .

Part of all of the above is ritual, and part of it is style. Baseball players

are slaves to rhythms. Hitting is timing. Pitching is upsetting timing, but pitching is also its own intricate, repeatable sequence of motions and pauses. Fielding is waiting and waiting and waiting and then running like hell. Against the screams of instinct, infielders must run *toward* balls that might bruise their shins or break their noses if they can't make the play. Outfielders must anticipate from the first moment of a ball's flight and the sound it makes when the bat hits it where it will come down, simultaneously deciding whether they can reach it while it is still in the air, whether they should play it on a hop, or whether they should leave the play to someone else entirely and return to waiting.

The preliminary rhythms—tapping the spikes of each foot twice or pulling at the cap and then the belt and then the cap again—are preparations for the acts themselves: pitching, hitting, fielding. So are the hundreds of adjustments the ballplayers make before we even see them. Their sanitary white socks must be just right, and the stirrups of their uniform stockings must not let too much or too little of the white show through. Some major leaguers (Steve Lyons comes to mind) wear black paint under their eyes to cut down the sun's glare even on days when they will almost certainly not be playing and on days when there is no sun. Major leaguers *care* about their uniforms to an extent that is unimaginable in any other professional game. After years with the Dodgers, years of wearing solidly traditional Dodger Blue each baseball day, Steve Garvey got traded to the San Diego Padres. The Padres, of course, had no tradition, and when it came to uniforms, they were trying to make a fashion statement. Their jerseys were brown, orange, and other assorted earth tones in odd, horizontal stripes. After he'd dressed in his new home team's colors, Garvey shook his head in dismay at his reflection in the clubhouse mirror. "I look like a taco," he said. It's not possible to imagine a basketball player or a football player saying something like that.

The necessary motions, the thoroughly adjusted socks, the eye black, and the rest are the elements of style, and the child ballplayer masters them long before he or she has learned to keep an eye on the ball. If you ever hear a former Little Leaguer deny that he or she has practiced swinging a bat in slow motion in front of a mirror while in full uniform, you will be in the presence of a liar. In baseball, style counts, and it comes only with practice. Whole teams of youngsters who cannot really play baseball yet will chatter and spit like champions. They will stretch like pros. They will stand at second base and wait as if it were no big deal to do so, even if they have never been to second base before.

Of course sometimes, through lack of practice or in times of insufficient concentration, they get it wrong. You know that has happened when you

see a second baseman standing at his position like a stork, scratching a mosquito bite behind his left knee with the toe of his right foot, or when the right fielder puts her glove on her head, extends her arms, and begins to spin in the grass, pretending to be a ballerina or a helicopter.

And then there is glove-biting. Some major league players still spit into their gloves from time to time, but they don't generally put their gloves into their mouths. Little Leaguers do, though. It's a breach of baseball style and etiquette that crosses barriers of race, gender, nationality, and culture. It's sort of funny to watch, unless the kid who's doing it is your kid.

High fives, low fives, and elbow-to-elbow salutes notwithstanding, nonchalance is crucial to baseball's style. The cliché has it that because baseball's season is long, it's no good to get too high or too low, no matter what happens on a given day. Striking out is only striking out, and hitting a home run is only hitting a home run. Either way, hundreds, maybe thousands, of at bats will follow. Veteran major leaguers sometimes achieve an almost

One of the things a ballplayer has to learn how to do is stand around. *Major League Tryout Camp, Nipper Mahar Field, Waltham, MA.*

Zen state of distance from the particular result of a moment of their work. These are the ones whose faces betray nothing when they have struck out or when they have utterly fooled and humbled a good hitter with a perfect pitch. But for true unconsciousness, the kids can make these guys look like amateurs. It is not unusual to hear one uniformed child on a Little League bench ask another, "What's the score?" or "Are we winning?" These are not furtive questions, but cheerful inquiries from folks who've simply sort of been elsewhere for an inning or two. To be that nonchalant is, of course, to go too far, and a coach overhearing such chatter is likely to scowl and say, "Let's get in the game." But staying in the game isn't easy. Even the pros goof sometimes and throw to second to start the double play when there are already two men out. The indiscretions of childhood are only more far ranging, more inventive, and louder. Once, in the midst of an inning full of walks, hit batters, and fumbled grounders in the infield, I heard a young outfielder yell, "Mom! I'm hungry! Did we bring sandwiches?"

It would be natural to conclude that such outbursts would end by about age thirteen and that certainly by high school every fielder would know that his role between pitches is to toss pebbles out of the way, work the dirt with his foot a little, and maybe shout, "Hawn, keed" or "Chuck fire" a time or two. But it is not so. Pat Jordan, the failed pitcher and successful writer, remembers a game in which one of his minor league teammates eschewed style spectacularly. Jordan, as was his custom, was walking the other team's batters around the bases on four pitches each. Runs were scoring at a stately pace, and nobody appeared to be paying much attention until the shortstop, whose affliction it was to care about the game, finally threw his glove into the dust, burst into tears, and shouted, "Throw strikes, goddamn you! Throw strikes!"

HITTING

"Relax and concentrate."

That is the advice you give a hitter. It's great, isn't it? How can you relax when you know, probably from experience, that the ball coming at you will hurt like hell if it hits you? How can you concentrate when a bunch of fielders are screaming something like, "No batta, no batta, no batta" at you? How can you relax *and* concentrate?

Hitting is a nest of mysteries, except when it is the simplest thing in the world. Some great hitters—Ted Williams and Rod Carew, for two—have written books on the subject. A lot of other great hitters have tossed the books aside and simply said, "I just try and see the ball, then hit it."

When they are "seeing the ball," hitters say it looks as big as a grapefruit, as big as a melon, as big as the moon. When they aren't seeing it, the ball looks like a pea or an aspirin tablet.

When you are a hitter, a pitcher can fool you in about fourteen different ways. He can throw you a change-up that looks just like his fastball for about fifty-seven feet, so that halfway through your swing you realize that the ball isn't there yet. He can break off a curve that will move like one of those remote control cars . . . there, and then not there at all anymore. Or you can fool yourself. You can guess fastball and get the slider, which will tie you up at the wrists or pull you across the plate like a water-skier tied to a boat driven by a man who's been stung by a bee. You can lean over the plate, guessing outside, and take one right in the ribs. You can promise yourself to take a first strike, and when you're not going well, it will be the best pitch you will ever see, every time you take it. You can go up determined to swing at the first decent pitch, in which case you will be a dead certain cinch to immediately wave at a fastball up in your eyes or a knuckler in the dirt.

Wade Boggs, the best hitter in the major leagues during the 1980s, was once asked if he could do anything to bring himself out of a slump. He shrugged. "You can be patient," he said.

Other hitters believe otherwise. In a slump, they will change bats,

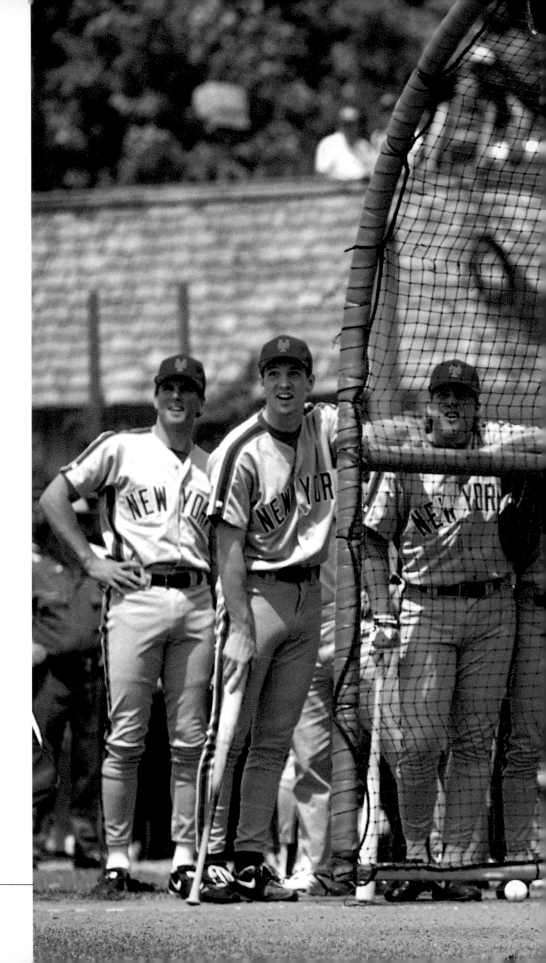

Batting practice is fun for almost everyone, but nobody has a better time at it
than pitchers, Dwight Gooden included.
Doubleday Field, Cooperstown, NY.

change clothes, or change their daily routines. Then, if they start hitting again, they will meticulously repeat the actions that brought back the charm. This is sometimes not easy. Tim Flannery, late of the San Diego Padres, once admitted that he couldn't wait for a fourteen-game hitting streak to end. "I'm superstitious," he said, "and every night after I got a hit, I ate Chinese food and drank tequila. I had to stop hitting or die."

Luck figures prominently throughout baseball, of course, and its influence is nowhere more evident than in hitting. You can guess right, see a pitch all the way, and whack it solidly, only to see it settle into somebody's soft hands for an out. You can swing like a man going after a rabid bat with a tennis racquet and bloop one over somebody's head or nick a spinning grounder into some Bermuda Triangle of the infield, where the pitcher, the shortstop, and the third baseman can only look at it as if a baseball was the very last thing they expected to find there.

But luck notwithstanding, hitting is discussed at length as science and as art. This is because it comforts man to approach the act as if it could be understood, even mastered. In this respect, the study of hitting is like theology. We can give names to all the mysteries of the cosmos, but finally we are on our own, supported, if we are supported at all, by our courage, our faith, and our wits. Anyone who is too smart for his own good, like Faustus, will end up on his ass in the dirt. Those who manage to retain their confidence, their humility, their health, and their batting eyes may be granted the extraordinary good fortune of success a little more than 30 percent of the time they get to the plate. If they can run, they may do a little better still by beating a throw to first base once a week on a ball that would have been an out if someone else had hit it.

This explains everything except the perfect feeling of achievement that comes with a ball hit on the nose to a place where nobody can catch it. Bang a fastball back up the middle past the pitcher, out over second base, and into center field, and you will know why so many fellows with bad knees are still playing park league ball, semipro ball, Municipal League fast-pitch softball, and so on down the line. You will know why Joe Jackson changed his name to Joe Johnson and Jack Joseph and whatever else he could think of and played ball in Georgia and all over the rest of the South after he'd been banned from organized baseball. Sometimes, he even wore a disguise. We will endure all sorts of indignities to be in the presence of the thing that brings us joy, and there are few joys as hard-earned and exceptional, albeit transitory, as that provided by a satisfactory at bat. A base hit is the evidence in motion that you have beaten the pitcher at what is nearly always his game, and it *feels* good, too . . . solid, right, and true. And then, as you start down the line toward first base, picking up speed

If balls fly free . . .
Why not we?   (With apologies to Bob Dylan)

Montana State Prison, Deer Lodge, MT.

Appearances notwithstanding, this is not Mark McGwire at age eight. You can tell because this kid is bunting. *Daisy Field, Boston, MA.*

as you go, you get to watch the scrambling and listen to the shouting your hit has caused. Then you pull up at first or make a quick decision, put your head down, and accelerate again, looking for another base or two. Everything is before you. The possibilities, at least for a moment, are many and wondrous. Small wonder that Reggie Jackson, who is by no means a stupid man, once said that he thought hitting was better than sex.

BATS

THE ALUMINUM BATS, shiny and indestructible, clank on the rack like a giant's gaudy wind chime. They have names like Thumper, Big Bang, and Super Stick.

"They're very pretty," I tell the clerk in the sporting goods store. "But haven't you got some wooden bats for adult softball players?"

The store spreads out over three large rooms and has everything else: sticks, clubs, gloves, and uniforms and caps in all colors and sizes. Jackets, wristbands, spikes, cleats, and skates. Soccer balls, footballs, baseballs, softballs, hockey pucks. But no wooden bats for anyone above Little League age, and not many for them.

"They're leftovers," the clerk says. "I'm not gonna carry them anymore after these are gone. The kids don't know they're supposed to hold the bat with the label facing them. Then, when the bats crack, they bring 'em in here and want their money back."

"But adults," I say to him, "those of us who grew up using wooden bats . . . we know about the label."

"It's not worth it," the clerk shrugs. "All the schools, all the organized teams . . . everybody wants aluminum bats now."

Or almost everybody. Up in Brownfield, Maine, the R. G. Johnson Company offers to serve the rest of us. They've been making wooden bats up there since 1927, one at a time . . . or two at a time, actually, because they have two lathes. One of them is the same lathe Rupert G. "Rupe" Johnson, the company's founder, saved from the fire that burned his house to the ground in 1938. In fact, the lathe and the special set of gouges Johnson used to make bats were the *only* things he saved from the fire, which suggests a major league commitment to his craft.

Bob Logan, Rupe Johnson's grandson, owns the company now, and though R. G. Johnson makes some commemorative bats for presentation to coaches at retirement dinners and like occasions, most of the lumber goes to people who actually use it.

"We used to get returns, too," John Leavitt, Bob Logan's only full-time employee, tells me. "Somebody'd crack the bat and then send it back because he thought it was defective. So, for a while now, we've been wrapping an instruction sheet around each bat we sell. It shows you how to hold it."

I don't remember who taught me how to hold a baseball bat. I suppose it was my father. I'm sure there were no written directions involved. I wish that were still the case. Written directions are for assembling swing sets and gas grills. We should learn how to hold a baseball bat properly from parents or older brothers or sisters or, at worst, from wise old coaches with gnarled hands and many stories—the sort of men who would no more pick up an aluminum bat than use a baseball glove for a lamp shade.

On the other hand, we live in a time for giving thanks at any good news, and as long as the two lathes in Brownfield keep turning, there will be some small portion of it for the users of wooden bats. And if our bats arrive with instructions for their use, who says we have to read them? We can cast them aside contemptuously, those of us who know the secrets . . . those of us who learned about baseball bats the way children once learned to hunt or make fire.

FANS

LATE IN 1991, Seattle Mariners owner Jeff Smulyan announced that his team was for sale. The asking price was $100 million.

I felt Mr. Smulyan would take $89.9 million. Interest rates were falling. I thought I saw an opportunity. Still, it was obvious that I wouldn't be able to swing the deal by myself. So, in a commentary for "Morning Edition," I announced my intention to buy the Mariners and asked everybody who thought that was a good idea to put $2.00 in an envelope and send it to me, c/o The People's Baseball Club. I promised that I would be a responsible owner and more. I'd change the team's name to the Seattle Baseball Players, so that nobody who made a living from the sea would be offended. I swore I'd trade any player who referred to himself in the third person. The dome would be history, and the fake turf would give way to grass. Roger Angell would write stories for the programs, so that if it did rain, folks could huddle in the few protected seats and chuckle appreciatively at his wit.

It was supposed to be a lark, but a lot of listeners were having none of that. Tricia Reeves from Conway, South Carolina, so appreciated my promise to sell rich, dark beer in the stands (but only to people who wouldn't get drunk) that she sent $25.00, enough, she hoped, "to buy a tiny piece of the team for myself and my four grandsons." Cameron Craigie from Tucson also sent a check, though he'd bristle at being considered a fan. "I hate baseball," he wrote, "but anyone who advocates tearing the top off the Kingdome can't be all bad." Anna Lee Adams from Campbellsville, Kentucky, offered to begin scouting locations for the Baseball Players' spring training site . . . all I'd have to do was cover her expenses. Another listener sent $2.00 to buy a piece of the Seattle team on behalf of her son, who was a Red Sox fan. "We've tried everything to save him," she said, "but nothing has worked. Perhaps if he *owned* another team . . ."

I shouldn't have been surprised. The best fans find beauty and truth and even therapy in their game. They may or may not love the home team, but they *certainly* love the enduring images, sights, smells, and sounds of the game. They listen to games on the radio and are happiest when a contemporary announcer's voice or expression reminds them of Red Barber, Mel Allen, or whoever brought baseball into the screened porches of their childhood.

And they take personally insults to baseball. In 1991, when the management of the Tigers dismissed longtime radio voice Ernie Harwell and started making noises about moving out of Tiger Stadium, a group of fans in Detroit began organizing against management and in favor of a kinder, gentler baseball. The Friends of Tiger Stadium set up temporary bleachers outside the ballpark on the last Opening Day of Harwell's employment with the Tigers. There they steadfastly listened to the game on portable radios. The same group submitted a beautiful, workable architectural plan for the renovation of Tiger Stadium and launched an energetic campaign to prove that the proposed relocation of the club was driven by greed and insensitivity and that then–general manager Bo Schembechler, previously revered as the University of Michigan's football coach, was in fact a blustering, dishonest clown. They published a newsletter, sold T-shirts, and staged a monstrous "hug-in" of Tiger Stadium . . . all to save baseball as they knew and loved it.

The common wisdom is that the best fans are in old baseball cities—Detroit, of course, and Boston, Chicago, New York, and other venues where the game has lived for at least a century or so. There is no doubt some truth to this line. The continuous presence of baseball in a place and the summer hum that touches even people who don't think they're paying attention help to make good fans.

But it isn't the only way. In minor league towns, there are people proud to claim allegiance to teams with names such as the Mudhens or the Dukes. Rooting for these clubs should be heartbreaking. Just when you get to know a player's face and begin to anticipate the extent of his promise, he is snatched away by the big club, where more likely than not, he will sit on the bench. No matter. Love knows no logic. In Winter Haven, Florida, where the Red Sox used to maintain an A-League team, the residents would fall all over each other asking the players home to Sunday cookouts. In the smallest parks, behind the most forlorn chicken wire fences, sit earnest, heavy, bespectacled boys with dog-eared notepads, keeping track of every pitch to every future truck driver and insurance salesman who is trying, for a time, to play baseball.

TY COBB called them bugs. He was once suspended for climbing into the stands to beat up a particularly vicious heckler, who turned out to be

crippled. The relationship between fans and professional players has often been difficult and worse. One school of thought has it that the age of the $1 million and $2 million and $7 million contract has put more distance than ever between the player on the field and the fellow in the stands whose dreams he bears. According to this theory, fans are now more inclined than ever to be abusive and violent, both because they feel cheated when the multimillionaires fail and because they can no longer identify at all with men still in their twenties who are financially secure for life. But that is the reasoning of a sociologist. It may not be wrong, but it is certainly incomplete. So much of what drives a fan is bound to elude even a soft science.

I have heard middle-aged men say they attend baseball games only to get away from their wives and their children. I have talked to young and not-so-young women who always buy seats behind home plate and close

On a summer night in a minor league town, you can go to the ball game or go to the movies. Why do you suppose anyone ever goes to the movies? J. P. Riddle Stadium, home of the Fayetteville Generals (South Atlantic League), Fayetteville, NC.

to the field because that is the best place for checking out the tight fit of the batter's pants as he stretches and preens before stepping into the box. Some children remember nothing of their first encounter with baseball but the popcorn and peanuts and the delicious thrill of dropping shells and empty paper cartons and cups at their feet without censure.

Some fans are obviously crazy. Major league players can only shake their heads at the repeaters . . . the people who are *always* in the parking lot or at the rail by the dugout with their autograph books. Some of them have hundreds of signatures from the same player, but they will entreat the man for his autograph again and again anyway, as if they are incapable of restraining themselves. Or perhaps they don't even distinguish between the players. Maybe their lives are so barren and dreary that brushing up against *anyone* whose significance has been certified by newspapers, radio, and television is the best they can manage. Major league baseball players are frequently crude and insensitive, but they are, by and large, more accessible than politicians or ax murderers, neither of whom have anything in their contracts about being civil to the public.

Some fans have made religion and myth of baseball. Annie Savoy, the fictional groupie in the movie *Bull Durham*, combined incense burning, the mystical properties of the number three, and something about how the Aztecs were supposed to have breathed through their eyelids to construct a faith with baseball at its center. Donald Hall wrote a short, convincing poem that presented Ted Williams as Achilles. It doesn't matter that most of the players might not know Achilles from Cookie Rojas. They are too busy playing baseball or preparing to play it to know much of anything else.

Most of the players are mystified by the fuss the fans make over them. The clubhouses and the dirt and the grass are no more magical to them than a courtroom is to a lawyer or an operating room to a surgeon. Baseball is their hard work. Even those who might have the inclination to dream on it don't have the opportunity, because dreaming requires distance. You don't dream about what you know. You cannot be lyrical and try to hit a ball coming at you at ninety miles an hour at the same time. And yet, there is room even here for the convert. Johnny Temple played second base for the Reds during the fifties and sixties, when the club's home park was Crosley Field. Crosley was demolished in 1972, but in 1988, a bunch of splendidly foolish people in Blue Ash, Ohio, who couldn't accept the loss of the park built a life-size replica of it, complete with the score of the last game the Reds played there. Johnny Temple, sixty years old, attended the dedication ceremony. "First I got goose bumps," he said of the experience, "then I cried." He had become a fan.

The wave in Caracas is the same as the wave in New York, Minneapolis, or San Diego,
except that in Caracas they also throw cups, which may or may not be filled with beer.
Estadio Universitario, Caracas, Venezuela.

*   *   *

DIFFERENT PARKS make for different fans. Everybody knows that pro baseball fans in southern California leave early. Whole crowds have walked out of no-hitters in progress. In Chicago's Wrigley Field, the fans in the bleachers derisively throw opposition home runs back onto the field. The fans in Montreal have a reputation for eating and singing and not really knowing what the hell they're seeing. In New York, numbers of people apparently pay their way into the ballpark just to ensure that somebody will be within punching distance that evening.

These generalizations are risky, of course, but they're also inescapable to some extent, as are some of the conclusions that have come to people who've gone further afield for their baseball. Pam Postema, who might have been the first female umpire in the major leagues if justice had been done, worked in Winter League ball for several seasons. She was sometimes propositioned and even received proposals of marriage while she was behind the plate. In the middle of one game in Venezuela, a paying customer threw an orange that hit Postema in the back of the head. She was told by team officials later that she'd been lucky, because the folks in that section usually threw rocks.

And it could have been worse, still. Four and five decades earlier, when Satchel Paige and numbers of other Negro League ballplayers were playing winter ball in Santo Domingo, games were sometimes interrupted by staccato bursts of machine-gun fire from the stands. Paige and his teammates would hit the ground and hug it until the umpires and the army had restored sufficient order for the game to continue. On the rare occasions when Paige's team, which was the personal franchise of Señor Trujillo, would lose, the dictator himself, accompanied by armed bodyguards, would meet with the players after the game to remind them that he hadn't brought them to the island to humiliate him. These performances were apparently sincere and convincing and should probably call into question North American claims that Bill Veeck, Tom Yawkey, and Gene Autry have been the game's most passionate owner/fans.

THE ADVANTAGES that baseball fans have over their counterparts in other games are marvelous and many. Baseball has history, and its numbers reflect myriad levels of achievement over time. Its players are human-size and easy to identify, and often we can see what they're thinking and feeling. With the exception of the catcher, they do not wear masks. Except when there is a rhubarb, which is really most often a dance, they do not bunch up into a scrum. Almost always there is a lot of distance between one base-ball player and another, and they all stand around a lot. This gives fans the opportunity to study them. Some Little Leaguers can mimic with wonderful accuracy the way their favorite pitcher glares at an umpire or their favorite hitter spits. In any ballpark, an old man will watch the shortstop for an inning or two and then tell you how there is a little Pee Wee Reese in him, or a little Luis Aparicio, or maybe a little Don Buddin.

This is not to say that baseball fans are invariably artists or historians or writers, though an awful lot of people in each category have counted themselves fans. It *is* perhaps to suggest that baseball's appeal to prospective fans is various. Action accounts for much of it, of course. But just as important are all that space and time within which to appreciate the action, take notes on it, commit it to memory. There is no other sport in which keeping score gives you the opportunity to recreate later every meaningful circumstance of the game. Thomas Boswell, one of the very best writers who has turned his talents to baseball, once wrote, "All baseball fans can be divided into two groups: those who come to batting practice and the others. Only those in the first category have much chance of amounting to anything." Boswell might have easily written the same thing about keeping score. Huge, colorful instant-replay screens might seem to render the cryptic, sometimes impenetrably idiosyncratic scribblings of all the amateur scorekeepers archaic; and sure, it's true that almost all old scorecards end up in the bottoms of desk drawers, never to be read again. But the first argument is only that television has superseded printed matter, and that is an argument for fans of pro football, a game that television made. The second rests on the supposition that the constantly exploding present of games, the next game and the next and the next that the sponsors and networks so constantly and loudly exhort us to watch, *must* be more crucial and exciting than whatever story some smudged and creased old scorecard can tell us. The real baseball fan isn't entirely convinced that this is true. He isn't ready to forget the games he's seen. He'd like to think about them a little. He would no more throw away his scorecard than an archeologist would toss out his field notes or a musicologist would burn her tapes. When he tells the story of the day he saw Luis Tiant pitch the opening game of a doubleheader and Juan Marichal pitch game two, he wants to be able to prove it happened . . . just give him a minute to find the right program, and you could look it up.

"HEY! SIGN THIS!
SIGN THIS!
GIMME A BALL!"

THERE ARE A LOT of good baseball autograph stories. In *A League of Their Own*, the movie loosely based on the long-defunct women's professional baseball league, Tom Hanks plays besotted former major leaguer Jimmy Duggan, whose signature still has some worth, at least to one short, fat, cherubic redheaded boy. Duggan takes the ball from the kid, smiles crookedly, and scrawls, "Avoid the clap, Jimmy Duggan."

Gaylord Perry, whose value as a celebrity and an autograph signer appreciated marvelously when he was finally elected to the Hall of Fame, was once discoursing on the prevalence of baseball card shows. To be fair, these events are not always depressing exercises in naked greed. A fellow I know talks about the time he went to one of the shows to meet Robin Roberts, the Hall of Fame pitcher whose cruel fate it was to be employed by the Phillies between 1948 and 1961. This fellow had brought along an old *Sporting News* article about Roberts as a phenom, and the retired pitcher happily read the whole thing while the line of people waiting for his autograph grew longer and longer. This fellow who'd brought the article explained to Robin Roberts that Roberts had been his favorite player and his father's favorite player, too. Roberts said he appreciated that and invited both father and son to visit with him when they were in the area again.

But Robin Roberts is an extraordinarily personable former player, and the scene my friend described with misty eyes is not representative. Almost everybody agrees that, all too often, the card shows are indefensible. Hundreds of kids with dollar signs in their unmisty eyes snake efficiently past signing ballplayers, many of whom don't even look up except to check the clock. Nobody seems to be having any fun except the promoter. But Gaylord Perry defended the practice in a drawl so full of charm it dripped. He spoke as if his subject was charity. "The shows are good," he said, smiling, "because there the kids know for sure who's signing that ball." This

Opposite: This field, home of the Boston Red Sox AAA team, is partially surrounded by a high, concrete wall. The dugouts are cut into the wall, and the players sit about ten feet below the first row of box seats, so autograph seekers have to fish for their prizes. In bottles that they've sliced open, they let down baseballs, pens, and messages like, "Please sign this for my little brother who's dying." Whoever came up with this curious design for a ballpark had a sense of humor. Or he hated kids. *McCoy Stadium, home of the Pawtucket Red Sox (International League), Pawtucket, RI.*

contention was marvelous for the image it evoked of hundreds of furtive and cloaked druidlike figures in dark cellars underneath the nation's ballparks, forging signatures as fast as they can, dropping them into unmarked crates for shipment around the world to dupes and gulls fourteen and under.

Since the coming of the card shows and the catalogs and the auctions of anything autographed by anybody, some players have come to think of their signatures as much too valuable to give away. But at the edge of the dugout before a game, there are still enough fellows signing to keep the kids coming back. Some of the children are authentic in their hero worship. Others are on the payrolls of adult memorabilia dealers, who tutor and direct their charges the way Fagin ran his band of juvenile thieves. There are even accounts of a few who have hobbled toward the field on unnecessary crutches or wearing fake casts in order to appear pathetic and deserving. Once I was drawn to a skinny, persistent kid with a voice like a dentist's drill. "Gimme a ball! Gimme a ball!" he kept screaming.

"How many baseballs have you got at home?" I asked him.

"Twenty-six," he said proudly.

On another day, this time at Fenway Park, I was sitting in the Red Sox dugout when then-manager Joe Morgan reached his saturation point with the little beggars who were leaning in from the box seats. Morgan finally banged the bat he was holding on the dugout's concrete steps and walked straight into the bleating. "What the hell's the matter with you kids?" he shouted. "When I was your age, I used to come to the park to see the game. I used to watch the players to learn how to play." For a moment there was silence among the children. Maybe at least some of them were thinking about our diminished times, repenting their mercenary frenzy, even if the rest were quiet only because they were so shocked that Joe Morgan was speaking to them at all. Then the moment ended. It must have occurred to Morgan that the kids didn't care why he'd once come to games. He turned his back on the box seats and stepped back into the dugout, shaking his head and muttering.

"Mike! Roger! Wade!" the kids began shouting again. "Sign this! Sign this!"

Joe Morgan's dismay notwithstanding, one can't entirely blame the kids. They are not stupid. Many of them read the collectors' catalogs and auction lists, which tell of astonishing prizes. A "George Brett Game Used Bat, showing a lot of tar, tape and use (cracked)" will go on the auction block at $180.00. It's not clear whether the bat would be priced even higher if it weren't cracked. Maybe a crack is a good thing. After all, in the same catalog, one of Casey Stengel's old baseball shirts is described as "dirt-stained," as if *that* is a good thing. The presumption, I suppose, is that the dirt came from a sacred place, perhaps a ballpark since torn down. Who would be interested in the shroud of Turin if at some point someone had washed it?

Happily for those who love stories, the lunatic baseball memorabilia market has led to some beauties. Six years after the ground ball that Mookie Wilson hit through Bill Buckner's legs in game six of the 1986 World Series squiggled malevolently into right field, it was offered at auction. Some wag called Buckner and asked if he'd join the bidding.

"I'll pass," Buckner said.

But his decision didn't hurt the market. An actor named Charlie Sheen, who'd pretended to be a baseball player in a couple of movies, paid ninety thousand dollars for the ball. There followed a debate about whether the ninety-thousand-dollar item was even the real thing. Buckner said he thought it wasn't. Mookie Wilson claimed he was sure it was. Clubhouse men testified amid a flurry of contradictory certificates of authenticity. Claims and counterclaims were exchanged. Too much attention was paid. And the strange and wonderful upshot of the whole business will probably be that Charlie Sheen's baseball will one day be sold for more than he paid for it, since there is no sign that the public's appetite for such things has been satisfied.

ALL THIS is not to suggest that there is no such thing in baseball as a relic of real value. Consider, for example, the relatively few souvenirs of the Negro Leagues, which during the long, stupid years of baseball's segregation, until 1947, employed some of the greatest players ever. In Cooperstown, and in the Negro League Museum in Kansas City, there are wonderful tin posters advertising Negro League all-star games and the Negro League World Series. Bats on display might have been used by Josh Gibson, Mule Suttles, and Turkey Stearns. There are black-and-white photographs of ballplayers whose names have been lost, though they would have had places in official record books if they had been white.

These mementos carry the weight of the shame of the past, but if you look at them more closely, they have more to say. The men who played in the Negro Leagues were proud of their skills and their ability to endure and prevail. With the exception of Satchel Paige, they didn't get rich. But they played with an enthusiasm that the wretched circumstances of bigotry couldn't, finally, diminish. When baseball fans look at what these ballplayers have left behind, they can be reminded not of a World Series lost through the legs of an unlucky first baseman, but of the persistence of several generations of players and club owners who managed to build com-

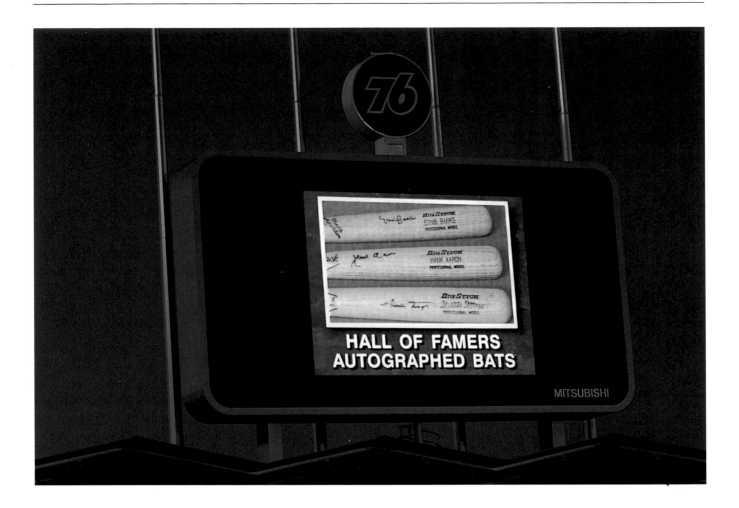

"Okay, okay, leave the park early if you must. But at least *buy* something before you go." *Dodger Stadium, Los Angeles, CA.*

petitive and popular baseball teams despite a white baseball establishment that was, at worst, vicious in its hostility and, at best, indifferent. In the little corner at Cooperstown devoted to the days of the Negro Leagues, fans can think about something more substantial than how small the fielders' gloves used to be. They can be reminded of man's perverse inhumanity to man as it has been reflected even in our games and of the ongoing struggle to put corrosive hatred and fear behind us.

THE PLACES
OF THE GAME

ONE OF THE MOST WELCOME and encouraging developments in baseball's recent history is the apparent rediscovery of how to build a ballpark. For several bleak decades, nobody seemed to care. The Astrodome in Houston, the Metrodome in Minneapolis, and the essentially interchangeable saucers in Cincinnati, St. Louis, and Philadelphia were the best the builders could do. They should have been locked away for lack of imagination and sins against the game.

The common excuse for these outrages against sense and sensibility was that the modern stadium had to be adaptable to more than one sport for owners to make a buck. Always, it seems, the demands of art and the requirements of business have banged up against each other within baseball. The game's greatest scandal, the tanking of the World Series by the Black Sox in 1919, was a direct result of White Sox owner Charles Comiskey's determination to swindle his players out of even the meager wages and bonuses he'd promised them. But during the 1980s, after much of the landscape had been pockmarked with stadia where the chief virtues were an outfield that could be vacuumed and parking that stretched for miles, numbers of owners got religion. In Chicago, the new Comiskey Park features not only modern amenities, but homage to the several old ballparks. In Baltimore, the Orioles moved into Oriole Park at Camden Yards, which was built on the site of a tavern that had been run by Babe Ruth's father. The place hummed with such righteous vibes that when Oriole shortstop Cal Ripken, Jr., took the field for the first time, he was moved to say, "I know this place is brand new, but it feels like they've been playing baseball here for a hundred years."

Needless to say, real grass covers the fields in the new homes of the White Sox and the Orioles. Astroturf and the noxious experiments that followed it were justified by their perpetrators as safer than the stuff upon which baseball had always been played. The innovators commissioned studies to demonstrate that fewer injuries would occur on the carpet than had on grass. The truth was that the new surfaces were ugly *and* dangerous.

An employee paid by the hour collects the baseballs that land in the net above the fabled Green Monster. Then they are probably sold to collectors for twice what the hourly employee makes in a year. *Fenway Park, Boston, MA.*

Outfielders began coming up with rug burns and a heretofore-unknown baseball malady called turf toe. Managers began holding players with bad knees or ankles out of games played on the mat as they recognized the damage the hard surfaces were doing. Players began talking about how the fake grass was shortening their careers. Meanwhile, ground balls hit on the new surfaces behaved, as Peter Gammons said, "like marbles in a bathtub." In the game's slack moments before innings began, fielders would sometimes bounce baseballs off the ground like tennis players getting ready to serve. Once the game was on again, innocent pop-ups that went uncaught would bounce once and leap like superballs over the heads of embarrassed outfielders.

Still, no doubt people from Toronto to Seattle and from Kansas City to Montreal feel for the ballparks there, artificial turf and all, the same veneration that old-timers feel for Ebbets Field, Baker Bowl, and Shibe Park. These are, of course, the people who saw their *first* big league games in these places, probably in the company of their fathers, and almost certainly through eyes as round and wide as pocket watches.

My own such initiation came on a July day in 1956 or '57, when the New York Giants were playing the Pirates at the Polo Grounds. My father had bought box seats, which seemed to me miraculously close to the action. As far as I was concerned, the twelve or twenty thousand folks in attendance that day were the luckiest people on earth. I got an autograph from Steve Ridzik, who won just one more game than he lost over the course of a twelve-year career, but who was all right with me. My mother or father took a picture of me at the ballpark that afternoon. It is mounted in a family scrapbook, and underneath the picture, someone wrote, "Giants win, 4–3. (Thank goodness.)"

Dodger Stadium,
Los Angeles, CA.

∗ ∗ ∗

AT THE TOP of the line, it works something like this. You drive through a couple of thundershowers on an unfamiliar highway to get to a ballpark you've never seen before. The purpose of the intermittent rain is to keep people who don't really care one way or the other away from the game. They will figure it might rain, off and on, all night, and they will wait for clear skies in the next homestand.

When you reach the stadium—and at the top of the line the place might be too small to really be called a stadium—parking spaces will be available within a block or two of the yard. Parking will cost a dollar.

You buy your single ticket from a fellow with plenty of them left to sell. "No batting practice because of the rain," he says, figuring that is the only explanation for your presence at the park an hour before game time. You smile and go in anyway.

There are plenty of seats up behind home plate. You find one directly above a row of old men who turn out to be scouts. During the game, they will fiddle with radar guns and make notes every once in a while about the players before them. Now, they are relaxing with each other, swapping stories. You listen to one about a shortstop who showed up at a scouting camp in Connecticut and fired the ball across the infield at ninety miles an hour, play after play.

"Ninety miles an hour?" says the scout who's listening. "Sounds like a pitcher."

"Yeah," says the scout telling the story. "That's what I told him. So now that's what he is." They both laugh.

There are more stories, and eventually one of the scouts catches you

Into the trees is a home run. Over the mountain is a hell of a story. *Hatcher Field, Anaconda, MT.*

Opposite above: Bowen Field, home of the Bluefield Orioles (Appalachian League), Bluefield, WV. Opposite below: Legion Park, home of the Great Falls Dodgers (Pioneer League), Great Falls, MT.

listening in. He smiles and says, "Come on down here with us, son. No sense in getting a stiff neck. What's your name? You look like a ballplayer."

You could live on that for a winter or two.

Half an hour before game time, the sky clears for good. A grounds crew made up of about equal parts old men and teenagers scuttles out from somewhere and starts the long process of removing the tarp. As they reveal the soft, dry dirt, you're aware, suddenly and again, of how bright the grass is, how perfect the contrast between the great, green lawn of the outfielders and the arc of the brown infield.

Recently, a book about some of the most wonderful places for playing baseball appeared. It is called *Green Cathedrals,* which is a nice title, but a little misleading. Some good settings for the game aren't even big enough to be called chapels, and some of them are lent beauty only by the power of memory and imagination. Constants exist, of course: the distance between the mound and the plate, the distance between the bases. Time weathers splendid quirks into more splendor: center field in the Polo Grounds, which went on forever and seemed to have been created on the off-chance that someday Willie Mays might be born and come to play it; the crooked wall in Ebbets Field. There is no reminder of baseball where those particular parks once stood, but sometimes the people who have torn down the yards have been less insensitive. When the smallish and thoroughly likable Forbes Field in Pittsburgh was demolished to make way for one of the ugly, concrete look-alikes, home plate was preserved under Lucite, and the section of the outfield wall over which Bill Mazeroski's World Series–winning home run soared on October 13, 1960, was saved, too.

The charms of smaller ballparks are for the most part smaller, but they are no less compelling. City leaguers and softball players in any town can take you from field to field, pointing out where their best shots landed or where they tore up their knees and first knew they would never play anywhere else. All ballparks that have stayed where they are for some time have history and ghosts. They all have stories, and the stories share the frame of the game—the foul lines and the harmony of three strikes, three outs, and nine innings. Quite often, the stories also share the presence of the fathers of the storytellers. Boys learn football from their coaches and basketball from their gym teachers, but they begin learning baseball from their fathers. They play catch in the backyard or in the park. Hence: "My father and I played catch here until it was too dark to see the ball, or until my mother came and got us. I'll bet if I hunted around in the attic, I could find my glove . . ."

So, here's a possibility to consider. Baseball fields are places of magic and wonder, even those that aren't cut out of Iowa cornfields, because they marry the elegance of geometry with the fascination of history (which is only a fancy name for story-telling) more effectively than any place but a church. Even on a sandlot, the geometry matters to baseball in a way that is true of no other sport. In football or basketball, out-of-bounds is nothing more interesting than out-of-bounds, whether the ball is in the road or in a patch of poison ivy. But on a ball field, if the trees in left are closer than the ones in right, you probably have to make up a rule: ground-rule double if you hit the trees in left . . . or over the street's a home run, because you don't want an enthusiastic outfielder to get hit by a car. Major leaguers now don't have to concern themselves with shifting rules, but at one time, they did. Photographs of the old parks show that greedy owners would sometimes sell patrons standing room along the foul lines and even in the outfield, particularly for postseason contests. Cheap home runs and doubles would sometimes decide these games, but the owner of the losing club was no doubt consoled by the knowledge that he and his colleague in the hustle had milked the afternoon for every dollar it could provide.

And, of course, in lots of pro ballparks the dimensions and qualities of the buildings created or create adventures that no football or basketball player will ever know. Fairness itself is flaunted by geography. In that same Polo Grounds where Willie Mays could run forever and haul in a shot such as the one Vic Wertz hit in the 1954 World Series, a batter could practically spit from home plate to the seats if he aimed down the right-field line. Even today, in Fenway Park, a hard line drive to left will often bang off the wall for a single, while a ball that would have been a routine fly anywhere else will drop softly into the net, a home run so cheap you'd think the batter might be embarrassed by it and offer to return to the plate and take it over.

Regarding the history, ball fields are like battlefields, except that nobody has to die. Every kid who played ball can show you a spot where she snatched one off her shoe tops, somersaulted, and came up with the ball, or where he hit one over the brook. Multiply that by a hundred or so, and you have the degree to which big leaguers can remember where their first home runs fell to earth or how many steps they took to get from first base to the dugout or how the dirt felt between their fingers when they picked a little of it up and then tossed it away and then stole second in a place that's a high-rise now. This is personal history, small stuff, but just as surely as the sandlot moments we remember, the deeds of Babe Ruth and Walter Johnson and Ty Cobb are associated with place.

Cal Ripken, Jr., a dancer for the Orioles. *Oriole Park at Camden Yards, Baltimore, MD.*

FIELDING

LET US BEGIN with the dubious proposition that there is such a thing as "a routine ground ball to short." All the shortstop has to do to fulfill his obligation in the dance of this particular routine is to scuttle into position so that he is squarely facing a ball, the direction of which he's had roughly half a second to predict; catch that ball, which may be heading for his toes, his ankles, or his knees and still be within the realm of "routine"; set himself and discover where he is in relation to first base; and throw the ball over there on a line true enough so that the first baseman, who also has to worry about a runner bearing down on him, will not be inconvenienced. This is a "routine" only because the people who perform it have practiced the elements of it so often that their muscles and nerves fall into the act without complaint or hesitation.

This is remarkable, but we have come to expect no less. We easily forgive hitters who fail more than seven out of every ten times they try to hit safely. We recognize philosophically that even on a good major league pitching staff, the number three starter will probably lose about as often as he wins. But the shortstop who boots a ground ball and the left fielder who misjudges a fly are clowns.

Nor are we alone in our judgment. Dave Stieb, Jim Palmer, and lots of other major league pitchers have been notorious for glaring or shouting at fielders who have kicked the ball around. We may understand that hitters invariably fall into slumps and pitchers must sometimes endure streaks of wildness and losing, but when a fielder fouls up a play more often than every once in a great while, we are liable to start talking about him as a klutz, a choke artist, a head case, a bum.

THE FLIP SIDE of fielding is that the best plays made by the Ozzie Smiths of the world are invariably the stuff of highlight films. The headlong dive behind second base, the successful off-balance throw from deep in the shortstop hole, and the long run by an outfielder who can stretch or slide to catch the ball at the end of a line only he can see . . . these plays will do more than any act of hitting or pitching to surprise us into a new understanding of what some of our fellow humans can do with their arms and legs and eyes. It's the great fielding play that makes us turn to the complete stranger in the next grandstand seat and ask, "Did you see that? Jeez! Did you see that?" We're looking to share the fun, of course, but we're also seeking reassurance. He can't have made that play, but he did, didn't he? And I saw it, didn't I? And you did, too.

Fielding is the most thoroughly learned of baseball's skills. Hard throwers are born rather than made, and everybody knows some players are blessed with a "natural" swing. But nobody comes into the world with the inclination to stay down on a grass cutter. Infielders have to learn not to flinch. Outfielders have to learn how to get a jump on a ball hit in the air. Children don't know these things, of course, and some Little League games are all grounders through somebody's legs and lazy fly balls misjudged into many extra bases. And, often enough to encourage us all, these things happen to big leaguers, too.

It is tempting to say that at least fielders can know that practice will improve them, and there is some truth to this assertion. Consider Wade Boggs: the third baseman who takes one hundred ground balls every day before anyone else shows up for batting practice will make himself a better third baseman. The outfielder who can find somebody to knock flies off the wall for an hour so he can learn to play the various caroms will make himself a better outfielder. But the fiendish truth is that demons haunt even the apparently relatively pedestrian business of fielding. Steve Sax, a second baseman with the Dodgers and later the Yankees, went through stretches in his career where he could not be counted on to throw the ball to first base after he'd picked it up. Sometimes his throws were on the mark, but often they weren't. No amount of practice seemed to help. Every ground ball to the right side was an adventure. Mackey Sasser, while a catcher with the Mets, could throw the ball anywhere but back to the pitcher. He could play professional baseball, but he could not play catch. His routine tosses would sail out toward second base or bounce in front of the mound. Coaches, psychiatrists, and hypnotists couldn't help much. Who can understand these things?

Here is fielding condensed.

When you are nine, a Cub Scout in the Cub Scout League, you are a third baseman. You have grown into the position. From a big-eyed, earnest but slow-footed kid with a lot more imagination than ability, you have matured into a starting player who is about half dependable and who can at least be counted on not to get into dirt fights with the subs on the bench. On one green and dusty Saturday afternoon, you are in the ready position at third, bent at the waist with your hands on your knees, probably chattering, confident that you are at least as good as anyone else on the team except the pitcher, who is a natural, and the shortstop, who is actually a little quick.

The pitcher swings into his motion, all long arms and skinny legs, and the batter lifts an infield pop-up your way. You do not remember now, many years later, whether there was sun to lose the ball in on that day. You do not remember whether you pounded your glove while you waited for the ball to come down. You *do* remember that you shouted, "I got it! I got it!" and that the other infielders and even the pitcher, who has been known to make sure of such outs by claiming any fly in the infield as his own, deferred to you this time. So you are alone under the ball as it descends, and alone, in the midst of the last, "I got it!" when it hits you square in the eye.

First comes the confusion. You had it, didn't you? Then comes the pain, which is terrible, and the humiliation, which is worse. After the initial terror, your parents come to view the occasion as a sort of rite of passage. They take a picture of you in your uniform while the skin around your eye is still blue, green, and yellow. Your expression in the photograph is prematurely wise. You have learned that you are not an infielder. The next time you come to practice, the coach hands you the catcher's equipment. He does not say, "We thought maybe you'd better have a mask on the next time you call for a pop-up." He does not have to.

Thirty-five years later, you arrive at a ball field not unlike the one on which the Cub Scout League games were played. It's evening this time. You grunt a little as you stretch before the game. You are hanging on now, the beneficiary of seniority. On nights when most of the other members of your team can make it, you are a designated hitter. When only nine guys show up, you can still play a competent second base, as long as the shortstop, who is twenty-two, understands that he must cover second if anyone tries to steal.

But on this particular night, the manager goofs. He writes into the lineup the name of the starting center fielder, who is not there yet. Then, at game time, he compounds the goof with panic. Having noticed that nobody is in center, he looks to the bench, sees you first, and directs you to the empty place. You run out to the utterly unfamiliar position on legs older than any center fielder's should ever be. Under the insufficient lights, you tap your glove and hope for strikeouts.

Kirby Puckett. *Minnesota Twins spring training, Tinker Field, Orlando, FL.*

Of course, they do not come. Anybody who has ever played the game knows that the ball always finds the fielder you try to hide. After two men are out in the first inning, somebody bangs one to center. It looks as if it's coming straight at you. You stand, much too flat-footed, and wait. The ball takes one hop in front of you and kicks on by like a squirrel that has changed its mind on the highway.

The next hitter lines another ball to center, higher, not as well hit as the one you botched. Any other outfielder would make the catch with nonchalance, even disdain. You approach the ball warily and take it on one soft hop. The next hitter, trying too hard to drive one to center, strikes out, and your inning is over. When you get back to the bench, the regular center fielder has arrived. "Sorry," he says. Nobody else says anything.

But between these days, between merit badges and bad knees, is another one you can remember just as well. In the city you've moved to in order to attend graduate school, you have discovered a pickup baseball game that begins early each Sunday morning and doesn't end until it's too dark to play. Whoever gets to each position first plays it. Rosters shift and settle and shift again during the day. On this particular spring Sunday, you are a shortstop. Why not? Nobody knows you here. All morning you are a shortstop, and against history and logic, you are superb. Game after game, you want the ball. Staying down feels as natural as spitting or scratching. How could you have ever bailed out on a grounder or let anything go between your legs? You make the routine plays look routine, and your throws are straight as string. Just before it's time to break for lunch, somebody hits a ball sharply to your right. Without thought, you snatch it out of the air bare-handed. The batter is so surprised he stops halfway to first. The first baseman laughs as he takes your throw. It is a day as mysterious as grace. The game has never before been so easy, and it never will be again. For good measure, when it's your turn to hit, you knock a couple of balls into the trees beyond left field. On both benches, people wonder who the hell you are and why you're not playing semipro somewhere.

FIELDING IS baseball's most relentless, unforgiving measure. Lots of pitchers lose their fastballs and hang on with curves and sliders. Lots of old sluggers can still hit the ball far enough so that it doesn't matter much how well they run. But the brief, peak time of a fielder requires his young legs and arm, wit and concentration enough for him to play the hitters where they ought to be played, will enough for him to practice constantly, and enough luck to ensure that somebody younger, faster, and stronger isn't coming up behind him too quickly during one of the stretches when his

stars are out of line. Yet, most fans take for granted the work that all but the flashiest fielders do. The ways of rating them are chronically unfair, penalizing those with the best range for making errors on balls that other fielders would never reach at all. Great fielders, especially infielders, are underrepresented in the Hall of Fame, and at least until recently, they have been underpaid compared to their colleagues who hit home runs or pitch. But the satisfactions of making the allegedly routine play well and occasionally making the play that you know you cannot have made are real and true. They are only quieter pleasures than the feel of the line drive you have hit over everything or the right pitch, chosen and delivered, for strike three. Of course you *know* this if you remember that day at the park when you could not miss anything—as I hope, somehow, you all do.

6-4-3. Barry Larkin is as good a 6 as any and better than most. *Candlestick Park, San Francisco, CA.*

Rainout, Men's Senior League Playoffs, Al Lang Field, St. Petersburg, FL.

RAIN

DELAY

FOR VARIOUS REASONS, the ballpark is a bad place to be when it rains. In most of the seats, you'll get wet, and you never know how long the umpires will take to decide what to do. Without a game to distract you while you're eating, you're going to realize that the food sold at the park is awful.

But if you are listening to a radio broadcast of the game at home or in your car, and if your team is blessed with play-by-play guys who know how to tell a story, a rain delay can be fine. Ernie Harwell, Ned Martin, Jim Woods, and various other baseball storytellers have been warm company to millions of baseball fans who so enjoyed their talk and their recollections that some of those fans probably *hoped* it would rain.

If I were a play-by-play guy, I would know enough not to completely trust my memory. I would keep a file of anecdotes and repeatable lines in a corner of my radio booth. Each winter, I'd review the literature of the game . . . books of poetry and fiction having to do with baseball, and *The Baseball Encyclopedia*, of course, and *Baseball's Greatest Quotations*. I'd try to recall what anecdotes I could from conversations at the bar or at the winter meetings. I'd scribble them down, too.

And then, when it began raining hard enough for the umpires to call out the ground crew with the tarpaulin, I'd push the cough button on my mike, clear my throat, and introduce the fans to a poem by Philip Dacey called "Mystery Baseball," which contains the lines:

One man rounds third base, pumping hard, and is never seen
    again.
Teammates and relatives wait years at the plate, uneasy, fearful.

On a lighter note, I'd read from the price list of an auction house in San Francisco, where a 1952 Mickey Mantle baseball card recently sold for more than forty thousand dollars. Then I'd say, "It's still a great country."

I'd open my file of baseball quotes to the "J" section and talk a little about how baseball has always appealed to writers because it's so lyrical.

Then I'd read what St. Louis Browns pitcher Sigmund Jakucki said in 1945, when Pete Gray, the only one-armed man ever to play in the big leagues, asked Jakucki for help with his shoes: "Tie your own goddam shoes, you one-armed son of a bitch," muttered the pitcher.

"Pure lyricism," I'd say.

I'd find more lines to fit more stories, too. If the discussion turned to the virtues of the new ballparks with their amenities and their easy parking, I'd remind folks of what former Detroit first baseman Darrell Evans wondered when he heard that Tiger Stadium might be the next old park to go: "Where will all the ghosts live?" Evans asked.

If it was still raining then, I'd read the entire transcript of Casey Stengel's testimony before the Senate subcommittee that was trying to decide whether baseball should be exempt from the antitrust laws. Here is a small part of that illustrious performance.

Senator Langer: "I want to know whether you intend to keep on monopolizing the world's championship in New York City?"

Mr. Stengel: "Well, I tell you. I got a little concern yesterday in the first three innings when I saw the three players I had gotten rid of, and I said when I lost nine, what am I going to do and when I had a couple of my players I thought so great of that did not do so good up to the sixth inning I was more confused, but I finally had to go and call on a young man in Baltimore that we don't own and the Yankees don't own him, and he is doing pretty good, and I would actually have to tell you that I think we are more the Greta Garbo type now from success."

I don't know what I'd say after that. I guess I'd hope that it was time to play baseball again.

RHUBARBS

BASEBALL IS A GAME for all seasons because even when it is too cold or too wet to play it, you can always argue about it. Columnists who are desperate for copy can always work up something about whether the designated hitter is a good idea or an insufferable act of blasphemy; whether relief pitchers should be eligible for the Cy Young Award; whether any pitcher should ever be named MVP; whether the arrival of plastic grass and domes killed baseball as we once knew it or whether it simply opened the good old game up to audiences who would otherwise have been left out of the fun; whether orange baseballs should have been given another chance; whether the advent of free agency destroyed forever the notion of a genuine home team whose players one might get to know gradually, over the course of their careers; whether the 1927 Yankees would have beaten the 1975 Reds; whether Ted Williams or Charlie Lau was the more brilliant hitting theorist; whether Pete Rose should be in the Hall of Fame; and, of course, who was the very best ever.

In the interest of freeing up thousands, perhaps millions, of hours that would otherwise have been spent in speculation over these questions, I've decided to provide the answers here. My apologies to all the columnists who'll have no subjects now. I hope they'll all take deep breaths and write instead about the folly of nuclear weapons and the necessity of a national commitment to a cleaner environment.

1. The adoption of the designated hitter rule by the American League was an act of near celestial kindness. It enabled hundreds of thousands of people to see Orlando Cepeda hit after Cepeda could no longer run or even bend his knees. He was still a wonderful hitter. The rule has also extended the baseball lives of many other wounded veterans in the major leagues, and its beneficence has trickled down into twilight leagues, city leagues, industrial leagues, fast-pitch softball leagues, and so on. In dirt parks, under bad lights, across the land, slow, fat old fellows can play on.

The argument against the DH is, of course, that it has eliminated from the game some of its strategic dimension. Managers who have a DH no longer have as many variables to consider when trying to determine how long to stay with a pitcher. The sacrifice of this concern is nothing compared to the extension of so many lives in baseball.

2. Relief pitchers should be able to win the Cy Young Award, unless and until baseball creates an equally prestigious award that would be limited to them, and maybe even beyond that time. Who can argue with the assertion that, on some teams, the most valuable and effective pitcher has been a guy who came out of the bullpen? Consider Elroy Face, Rollie Fingers, and Dennis Eckersley in his second baseball life. Isn't the logical extension of this assertion that in some years the best pitcher, period, is a guy who comes out of the bullpen? Why should such fellows be penalized because at some point in their careers some manager or coach decided they should finish rather than start?

3. Pitchers should be eligible to win the MVP, except for Roger Clemens, who forever forfeited his right when he went around signing baseballs: "Roger Clemens—Cy Young, MVP" for a year after he won both.

4. Domes and fake grass are to ballparks as pornography is to love.

5. The orange baseball was a stupid and frivolous idea. So were the orange golf ball and the orange tennis ball. The orange basketball and the orange football are okay.

6. While it's a shame that players now move from team to team so often that children can't develop attachments to many of them, a civil right is a civil right. Even millionaires are entitled.

7. The '75 Reds would have beaten the '27 Yankees, 6–5, in ten innings. Don Gullett would have won it, and then he'd never have been heard of again. Johnny Bench would have doubled in the winning run after Joe Morgan blooped a single into center and then stole second base. Babe Ruth would have hit two solo homers, and Lou Gehrig would have knocked in the other three New York runs. Waite Hoyt would have taken the loss. (It's also interesting to ask what the 1918 Red Sox would have done against the '27 Yankees. The answer is that Babe Ruth would have struck out Babe Ruth in the bottom of the ninth to nail down the win for Boston.)

8. Ted Williams was a terrific hitting coach for Ted Williams. Charlie Lau and Walt Hriniak are the right coaches for almost everybody else.

9. Pete Rose's qualities apparently include crudity; dishonesty; an addiction to gambling, which he denied for a while, later admitted, and then denied again; an unprecedented inclination toward self-aggrandizement; reckless and insensitive disregard for his first wife's feelings; and a variety

Walter Hriniak is the hardest-working, most devoted hitting coach in the big leagues.
Chain O'Lakes Park, Winter Haven, FL.

Roger Clemens, Father Son/Daughter Game. *Fenway Park, Boston, MA.*

of other, lesser misdemeanors. But the Hall of Fame is the Hall of Fame, not the hall of virtue, or the hall of role-modelship. The place is full of drunks, gamblers, and slobs who could hit, run, and throw. Pete Rose, who accumulated more base hits than anyone else who ever played the game, should be in there, too.

10. Willie Mays was the very best ever.

PLAYERS AND THEIR MOMENTS: JOHNNY PESKY AND LUIS TIANT

JOHNNY PESKY played shortstop and third base very well for the Red Sox for a little over seven seasons. Later on, he coached, managed, and scouted for them. He did radio and television play-by-play work when they needed somebody for that. At seventy-three, he was still hitting ground balls to Boston's infielders, a company man.

Luis Tiant began his major league career with Cleveland. In 1968, he led the American League with an ERA of 1.60 and won twenty-one games. A year later he *lost* twenty games and the Indians cut him loose. He went 7–3 for Minnesota the following season, then got cut loose again. He was a fastball pitcher who could no longer throw much of a fastball. Boston signed him a year later, inexplicably stuck with him after a 1–7 season, and then found that against all odds, they'd come up with a gem. Over the next seven years, Luis Tiant won twenty or more games three times. He was, by all accounts, the soul of the team that made it to the seventh game of the World Series against the Cincinnati Reds in 1975. Then, as the club has done often enough to make sobbing the music of the Hub, the Red Sox spat into the eye of karma. The front office refused to offer Tiant more than a one-year contract, and he found employment with the Yankees and won thirteen games for them. When he was forty-two, Tiant retired as a pitcher and let it be known that he would very much like to work for the Red Sox in some other capacity. The phone never rang.

It can go either way, but in big league baseball, it's a good deal more likely to go your way if you are Johnny Pesky rather than Luis Tiant, especially in the days following your usefulness as a shortstop or a pitcher.

Tiant was born in Cuba, where his father was a legendary *lanzador* ("pitcher"). Luis Tiant, Sr., was supposed to have had a pickoff move so baffling that when he threw to first, batters frequently swung. His son, no less tricky than the old man once his fastball was gone, could deliver the ball from about nine different angles. At the top of one of his pitching motions, he looked like a man who had forgotten pitching altogether and had decided to count the stars. In the middle of another, he was a little boy peeking around the corner of December 25th to see if Santa had arrived.

Johnny Pesky led the American League in hits three times, posting averages of .331, .335, and .324. If he'd had even one year like that after 1975, he'd have been able to sign a contract that would have erased any possibility that he'd ever be hitting ground balls to anybody at the age of seventy-three unless he really felt like it. Of course, by 1975, Pesky had been retired as a player for twenty years. Still, if the prime of his career hadn't been interrupted by three years in the service, he'd probably be in the Hall of Fame. He should be remembered as a heck of a player. Instead, he is remembered primarily for a play that embodied the macabre tendency of the Red Sox to find a way to lose when it matters most. In the seventh game of the 1946 World Series, Enos Slaughter, of the Cardinals, scored the deciding run on a hit by Harry Walker. Slaughter came home all the way from first base, and there are those who say he'd never have made it if Johnny Pesky hadn't held the ball a fraction of a second too long before making the relay. There are also those, Pesky among them, who say that is nonsense, but *The Baseball Encyclopedia* identifies Johnny Pesky as the goat.

Luis Tiant is remembered primarily as a champion at combining an infectious sense of fun with an iron will to win, a rare and complex achievement for which his teammates loved him. In the fourth game of the 1975 World Series, Tiant, who acknowledged that his stuff on the mound was "bool cheat" that night, needed 172 pitches to beat the Reds, who had two runners on base in each of the last six innings and couldn't score. Carl Yastrzemski said of El Tiante that he "defended a one-run lead as if it were his family."

It is oversimple and not entirely fair to suggest that the propensity of the Red Sox to retain the Johnny Peskys of the world and pass on the Luis Tiants explains the failure of the franchise to win a World Series since 1918. Johnny Pesky is too nice a man: a cheerful, outgoing storyteller who is particularly kind to outsiders in a business where that's unusual. He's a fine fellow to have on your side. But it is a shame that there has not also been room for El Tiante . . . the mustachioed prankster, the elfin master of magic reality on the mound, the little fat guy who somehow got everybody out and then couldn't catch on with the club when his playing days were done.

There is a suggestion of the near-inevitable cruelty of an athlete's career in considering these two together, even though Pesky is a lifer and Tiant is not. If he is still banging out grounders an hour before game time when he is one hundred, Pesky can look forward to one more eager reporter

ready with the question about whether he held the ball. And, even if the writers who vote on admission to the Hall of Fame somehow find the wisdom to factor heart into their deliberations and choose Tiant for immortality, the pitcher who lost his Boston-area house to the banks sixteen years after he could have been king of the city is not likely to forget that the door to Fenway Park shut behind him forever on the last day he wore a uniform there. Even while the crowds are still cheering, the greatest careers are often seasoned with irony. And, when the cheering stops, the irony is sometimes all that's left. Perhaps the best, most shining feature of these two old ballplayers is that, on some days, each can still feel like singing.

Johnny Pesky: 1942–1954, Bos., Det., Was., .307. Luis Tiant: 1964–1982, Cle., Min., Bos., N.Y., Pit., Cal., 229–172. *Red Sox Fantasy Camp, Chain O'Lakes Park, Winter Haven, FL.*

Brewster White Caps players, Cape Cod League. *Eldredge Park, Orleans, MA.*

AMATEUR
BALL

BOB POWERS, the president of the Boston Park League and manager of the team sponsored by a bar called Great Scott, is also the league's most energetic promoter. "This thing began in 1929," he'll tell you. "It's lasted through a World War, Korea, and Vietnam. We've got guys who've gone from here to pro ball, and pros who've come back to play here when they were headed in the other direction. It's one of the oldest continuing amateur leagues in the country, and we like to think it's the best."

On the night I dropped by the ballpark at Cleveland Circle to see Great Scott and Palmer Mobil battle for fifth place, it wasn't. In the first inning, the Great Scott third baseman tried to take a ground ball sidesaddle and missed it. Then two Palmer Mobil outfielders lost line-drive singles in the lights, or lack of same, and each hit went for extra bases. At the end of two innings, it looked as if the final score might be about 16–15, and the winner would be the team that still had a pitcher left.

In the later going, both sides would settle down. Great Scott would win the game, 9–6. But that is beside the point. Admission was free, and the parking was easy. Somewhere out beyond the trees in right field, a saxophone player was blowing delicate, mournful riffs at the sky. When he eventually strolled into view, you could see he was wearing a baseball cap. Maybe he was playing an anthem to his own lost career. He was good, except that sometimes he stopped in funny places—to watch the game, I guess.

The spectators were uniformly charitable. Nobody hooted at errors or wild pitches. Applause followed each base hit. At the far end of the cracked concrete steps that made the bleachers, a row of old guys lounged around a portable radio tuned to the Red Sox . . . two games for the price of none. Closer to home plate sat a wiry young man who turned out to be Rodger Hebert, formerly a pitcher for Bob Powers and the Great Scott team.

"I pitched in '83, '84, and '85," he told me, as the saxophone started wailing again. "It was fun. We won. And it's nice playing for a team sponsored by a bar. They were good to us."

"Did you play against anybody who went on to the bigs?" I asked him.

"Sort of," he smiled. "I was a park league all-star in '84. We played the U.S. Olympic team in Fenway Park. I saw Will Clark hit three home runs . . . one to left, one to center, one to right."

"You give up any of them?"

"Nah," Rodger Hebert smiled. "I didn't even get into the game. But I did pretty well in the park league. I came along at the right time. In my first year, Bob Powers was so desperate for pitching he tried to do it himself. He'd pitched earlier for a number of years. He came out of retirement for one game, got hammered for an inning or two, and went right back into retirement."

I glanced at Powers, coaching at third base. He could certainly have passed for a major league coach, flashing signs, digging in the dirt with the toe of his spikes, shouting, "Here we go, Here we go . . . Coupla hits, coupla runs . . ." In his cheek was a chaw of tobacco the size of a golf ball.

"You think he stays with this just so he'll have a place to spit tobacco?" I asked Hebert.

"Could be just that," the former pitcher said.

"Do you get back here a lot to see these guys play?"

"No," he said. "I haven't been back in a bunch of years. But when Powers saw me tonight, the first thing he asked me was, 'Can you still throw?'"

"Can you?" I asked.

"Well," Hebert said, "in my mind I can."

As in our minds a lot of us can, and perhaps no place is more fit for the dreaming on it than the ball field before me that night. The same player could be brilliant and awful on successive plays. Nearly anyone who has played the game can remember the experience in those terms. But the soft night and the saxophone invited Rodger Hebert to recall his *best* days on the mound, and surely he was not alone in that respect. If I came to enough park league games, maybe Bob Powers or somebody else on the bench would look around in the late innings and ask me if *I* could still throw. It could not happen in Fenway Park, of course, but here? That is perhaps what the park league and the hundred leagues like it are for.

A STEP AND A HALF up and one area code east of the park league is the Cape Cod League. Here, it is a lock that you will see future pros. The league is partly underwritten by Major League Baseball, which explains why the clubs in it are flush enough to afford wooden bats. The players come from Pepperdine, Eckerd, LSU, and most of the rest of the best base-ball schools in the country, and more than half of them will eventually sign professional contracts. Each game program lists the players in the bigs who once played on the Cape . . . Carlton Fisk, Jeff Bagwell, Glenn Davis, Charlie Hough, Bobby Witt, and so on. There are also much longer lists of fellows still laboring in A, Double-A, or Triple-A Ball. Unlike the park league, nobody in the Cape League is on his way down.

Still, there is room here for the funky, and even with major league sup-port, there are no frills in the Cape League. Before each game begins, the public address announcer asks the fans to throw foul balls that leave the field back to the umpire. The players rake the infield themselves. In the fifth inning, somebody always passes a hat for contributions to keep the whole business solvent.

After the game, the players usually dine on submarine sandwiches that members of the team's booster club have made at home. Before the game, they play a scratchy tape of the National Anthem, except when the tape machine doesn't work. That's what happened at a rare weekday afternoon encounter between the Chatham Athletics and the Orleans Cardinals. For a few long moments, everyone at the park stood at silent attention. Eventually, some grumbling could be heard in the old wooden press box/announcer's booth that stands like a garden shed above the bleachers. Then Frank House, the public address announcer, began climbing deliberately down toward the field. Fans who hadn't previously attended Chatham A's games were briefly mystified, but the players knew at once what was going on. "Go get 'em, Frank," one of them said.

House, somewhat stooped and probably seventy, made his way toward a spot partway up the third baseline. He looked like he knew exactly where he was going. Once there, he turned and addressed the small afternoon crowd.

"Technical difficulties prevent us from playing 'The Star-Spangled Banner' this afternoon," he said. "I hope you will all join me in singing it, instead."

Everybody smiled. Most people joined in the singing, but we sounded a little frail, a little small in all the sunshine and open space—which didn't bother Frank House. He sang loudly. Duty had called, and he had answered. When the anthem was over, he bowed his balding head, raised his baseball cap in his right hand, waved once at the applauding crowd, and climbed up the bleachers, back to work.

Some fans come early, so they'll see batting and fielding practice. Some fans stay until the last out is recorded. The best fans do both. *Boston Park League, Kelly Field, Hyde Park, MA.*

Send out to central casting for a third-base coach, and they will almost certainly send back Bob Powers of the Great Scots. *Boston Park League, Cassidy Baseball Diamond, Brighton, MA.*

I saw that game with my daughter Amy, then just shy of six. She watched happily as long as our snacks and fruit juice held out. She'd seen a few innings of a minor league game a little over a year earlier. She'd seen the Red Sox on television a couple of times. I sat under that blue sky of that splendid Cape Cod day and watched her watching baseball. Maybe it would take.

And it might have worked very well. I had decided beforehand that I'd leave the game at the first indication that Amy'd had enough. When she gave the word, we'd walk into town in search of souvenirs. (Another quirk of the Cape League is an ordinance that prevents the sale of caps, T-shirts, or other baseball baubles at the park.) But the Orleans pitcher messed up the plan. He was wild high early in the game. In the second inning, he hit Chatham's Paul Petrulis (5 feet 10 inches, 155 pounds, Mississippi State) in the face with a fastball. Petrulis went down hard and curled into a ball at the plate. He was quickly surrounded by coaches, umpires, and players. Somebody waved up toward the press box, and Frank House growled a plea for help into his microphone. "Could we have the ambulance down here on the field, please?" he said. "Ambulance to the ball field right away, please."

In front of the firehouse, which sits on a rise beyond right field and across the street, there was some movement. Eventually, the ambulance rolled out of the garage, turned left, and disappeared behind some trees.

"Why don't they just drive down the hill?" Amy asked.

"Maybe it's too steep," I said, but I was wondering the same thing myself. Taking a baseball in the head is no joke. I thought of Tony Conigliaro.

All around us, people watched Paul Petrulis, hoping he'd get up, or at least move a little.

"Does this happen a lot?" Amy asked.

"Not a lot," I told her. "Hardly ever." I remembered a woman I know who, on her first trip to a racetrack, saw a horse collapse of a heart attack at the three-quarter pole and fall dead. She never went back.

"I'm sure he'll be okay," I said.

Fortunately, he was. Just before the ambulance crew arrived, Paul Petrulis stood up, holding an ice bag to his face. After a short consultation in front of the dugout, somebody must have decided the ambulance wasn't necessary after all. Petrulis and one of the coaches left the field, passing close enough so that Amy and I could see that the hit batsman was smiling. He would go to the hospital so they could take a look at him, but he would go in the coach's car.

"How's your nose?" somebody shouted.

"Okay, I guess," Petrulis said. "It wasn't much before this. No loss."

We watched another inning. The sun kept shining. Nobody else got hurt. Baseball had assumed again its pastoral disguise. Eventually Amy and I made the walk into town. At the store that specialized in Chatham A's memorabilia, Amy passed on the shirts, caps, and pennants. She chose an enameled pin featuring the new A's insignia: a smiling elephant clutching a baseball bat in its trunk while balancing on a baseball that said Cape League. When we got home, my wife greeted us at the door. "How was the game?" she asked.

"Good," said Amy. "See? I got this pin."

Nobody mentioned blood or the fastball up and in.

An hour and a half later, looking for something to do until it was time to eat dinner, the three of us and Alison, who'd been napping earlier, drove to the playground that was next to the ballpark. Remarkably, the game was still in progress. It had gone into extra innings. The crowd was smaller now. My wife went with Alison to the swings. Amy stood with me for a while next to the chain-link fence along the right-field line, watching from a distance the same game we'd watched earlier from the good seats behind the plate. After a while, Amy left my side and climbed onto the monkey bars a few yards away. She hooked her knees over one of the bars and hung upside down. From that position, she addressed me.

"Sometimes baseball seems like it goes on forever," she said.

She had begun to learn.

BASEBALL MAN

LENNIE MERULLO is a baseball man.

He was born in East Boston in 1917, the seventh of twelve children. Among his early memories is the clear sound of his mother's relentless question: "*Quando troverai un lavoro?*" ("When are you gonna get a job?") Each time he heard it, Lennie would grab his glove and head out the door, looking for a ball game. He always found one.

He was, by his own admission, a pretty fair infielder. "I was a good guy to have on your team," he says. "A shortstop"—he says it "shatstap" . . . always has—"and I could pick up the ball and throw it. And I was a little bit of a holler guy, too. I could keep people loose a little."

By the time he was in high school, Lennie was nearly six feet tall and rangy, as they say. He looked like a ballplayer, which is another thing they say. He so impressed Ralph Wheeler, a sportswriter for the *Boston Herald*, that Wheeler approached Lennie after a high school game one afternoon in East Boston and asked him what courses he was taking in school.

"I was taking the commercial courses," Lennie says, "and that's what I told him. He said that was too bad, because if I was taking the right courses, I could go to college on a baseball scholarship. I couldn't believe any of it. Nobody in my family was going to college.

"But Ralph Wheeler said he wanted to come over to the apartment some evening to talk to my parents. I said, 'Jeez, you don't want to do that, Mr. Wheeler. They'll throw you right out.'"

Wheeler persevered. He got Lennie to apply for a postgraduate year at St. John's Prep so that he'd have the academic background he'd need to attend Villanova. He was also serious enough to take the boy down to Braves Field when the Cubs came in to play the Braves, because besides being a newspaperman, Wheeler was an unofficial bird dog for the Cubs . . . a fellow who looked around for ballplayers and called Mr. Wrigley in Chicago when he saw a prospect.

"He took me over there a couple of times," Lennie remembers. "They'd take me to the visitors' locker room and give me spikes and a uniform that

Lennie Merullo, Baseball Man, at work.
Major League Tryout Camp, Palmer Field, Middletown, CT.

never fit. This was a few hours before the game, so sometimes there'd be nobody in there. But once, Babe Ruth, who was with the Braves then, was over talking to some of the Chicago players. He was up on a stool with a towel around his waist and a hot dog in his hand. He looked like he weighed three hundred fifty pounds. Anyway, I'd go out on the field and run around a little and then come back into the locker room, and by then all the players would be there . . . the Cubs.

"Oh, gee, I was so shy with them, I never talked to anybody, just maybe said 'hello,' whatever. You gotta remember I was a fifteen-year-old senior in high school. They'd give us double promotions in those days so we could get out to work earlier and help our families. I wasn't in any hurry, of course. I tried to fail my senior year so I could play some more high school ball, but they caught on and made me graduate."

The year in prep school did the job as far as academics went. Lennie and his family understood that he had a scholarship, and of course he played ball there. Years later, he found out that Ralph Wheeler had paid half the bill out of his own pocket.

Villanova was fine, too, but one day about six months before he'd finished his senior year, Lennie got a wire. It said he should take the train to Chicago and report to the offices of the Cubs. Classes were almost over. It was coming on toward Christmas. Lennie got on the train.

When he reached the station in Chicago, he was met by Bill Veeck, Jr. Years later, Veeck would own the St. Louis Browns and, after that, the Indians, and then the White Sox. He would run each team on laughably short money and with more imagination and energy than any owner had ever mustered before or has since. But when he met Lennie Merullo's train, Veeck was working for his father, who was working for Mr. Wrigley. Together, Lennie and Veeck, Jr., proceeded to the Cubs' offices in the Wrigley Building at 410 Michigan Avenue.

If Lennie Merullo had been shy in front of the Cubs, he was tongue-tied nearly to the point of paralysis in the presence of Philip Wrigley. So Mr. Wrigley did the talking.

"Leonard," he told his guest, "they say you're a fine ballplayer. And I'm told you're also a fine young man."

"Thank you," Lennie said.

"We can't ask you to sign with us, of course, since you're still in college. But I'd very much like to give you something to indicate our interest in you and in your progress. We know you come from a large family. We'd like to help you out." Here, Mr. Wrigley slid an envelope across his desk. Lennie Merullo looked at it for a moment before realizing that he was supposed to pick it up and put it in his pocket. Then he did so.

"Now that's done," said Mr. Wrigley, and he turned to one of the other young men in the office. "I've got two tickets for the Blackhawks-Bruins game tonight," he said. "Why don't you and Leonard go? And on your way over, stop off in the shops and buy Leonard some clothes for the trip home."

"I remember the coat," Lennie says. "It was chocolate brown, warm enough to live in. And they bought me a new hat and a beautiful pair of shoes. I came home to Boston looking about as sharp as I thought anybody could look. And I didn't just walk in the door when I got there. I wanted to surprise everybody. I knocked. One of my brothers answered the door, and everybody was sitting at the kitchen table. I stood there and they didn't know who I was. Finally, my mother recognized me, and she shrieked. I guess maybe she figured I'd stolen the coat.

"I told them I'd been to Chicago to meet Mr. Wrigley, who owned the Cubs. I told them that's where the clothes had come from. Then I put the envelope down on the table in front of my mother, and she opened it up, but she didn't know what a check was. She was holding fifteen hundred dollars in her hand, but she didn't know it. My brother had to explain it to her. Her eyes got wide then, and she looked at all the other boys around the table and said, *'Perche state qui facendo niente? Andate voi a giocare il baseball!'* ('Why are you sitting around here doing nothing? Go out and play baseball!')."

The following February, Lennie Merullo reported to Chicago's spring training camp. He started eager. He threw the ball across the infield as if he were trying to burn a hole in the first baseman's glove. A day later, his arm was so sore he couldn't pick up a ball. His career might have ended right there, except that, as Philip Wrigley had said, he was a fine young man as well as a pretty good ballplayer. People kind of liked having him around.

The Cubs carried him until the arm recovered. He played 7 games at shortstop for them in 1941. The next year, he played 143 games and had 132 hits . . . his major league highs. He was, by most accounts, serviceable: a fellow who would make the plays for you and wouldn't embarrass you at the plate.

"I did 'em some good," Lennie says. "I had a hard time relaxing myself. I used to get too tense to be a great player, but I could help the other guys out. And I could room with Phil Cavarretta, who was the greatest player those Cub teams had . . . hit .293 lifetime in twenty-two years in the big leagues, hit over .400 in a couple of World Series. But nobody else could live with him. He really could be a bear. When they let me go in '49, that's what they said to me. 'Who the hell are we gonna get to room with Phil Cavarretta?'"

When the Cubs released him, Lennie Merullo left casual fans two moments by which to remember him. One involved a short and bloody fight with Dixie Walker of the Dodgers, and Lennie prefers not to talk much about it, though it made all the papers at the time. The other earned him his only major league record, and he'll talk about it for as long as anyone will listen, which is a tribute to his sense of humor and his humility. On September 13, 1942, at the same Braves Field where Lennie had gaped at the Cubs as a teenager, he committed four errors in the same inning. No major league shortstop had ever done it before. None has done it since.

"My wife was due to deliver our first child," Lennie remembers. "I'd been up all night for two nights, one of 'em traveling from Chicago. And then the baby came early in the morning on the day of that game, so I went right from the hospital to the ballpark. And, of course, I was a father for the first time.

"I think one of the errors was a ground ball that I missed and two of 'em were throws . . . I'm not sure. I wasn't counting 'em, but somebody else certainly was. Anyway, the next morning, they had it in the paper like this: 'Merullo Boots Four, Son Born.' That one's been called 'Boots' ever since. But I'll tell you the one thing nobody remembers about that day. We won the game."

The inning of the four errors lived. Long after Lennie Merullo had retired, a cereal company called to ask permission to put his picture on a box of something. He was in the company of a football player who'd run the wrong way and scored a touchdown for the other team. Chicago columnist Mike Royko got a lot of mileage out of Lennie's errors, too. He wrote several columns about himself as a young Cubs fan whose life had been twisted into bitterness and irony by the hometown shortstop's hands of stone.

By contrast, Lennie's own life was happily untwisted. His experience in the big leagues confirmed something he'd known intuitively since the days he'd dodged a paper route or yard work in favor of pickup ball games. Baseball was what he wanted to keep doing. The Cubs recognized that desire as the primary requisite for continuing employment and offered him a job as a scout. Lennie signed on, but he also kept playing. Back home in Massachusetts, he joined a team in the semipro Blackstone Valley League. Evidence of his prowess there is only anecdotal, and one anecdote will suffice. Former Red Sox manager Joe Morgan once told of a day forty years ago upon which his brother, a shortstop who'd been trying to catch on with a Blackstone Valley team, returned home with a long face.

"What happened?" Joe asked. "You couldn't cut it?"

"Naw," his brother complained. "They got some old guy named Merullo out there and, man, he never misses."

WHEN THE MAJOR LEAGUE teams combined their energies to cut expenses and created the Scouting Bureau, Lennie Merullo went to work there. It gave him an opportunity to stay closer to home, but otherwise nothing changed. Into his sixties and his seventies, he has continued to run the tryout camps at which a couple of hundred hopeful kids run, throw, and hit while most of the scouts look on impassively and make minimal, cryptic notes. In a baseball undershirt and baseball pants, Lennie watches the outfielders until he can't stand it anymore. Then he grabs the ball away from some kid fifty years his junior and says, "Jeez, ya *look* like a ball-player. Why don't ya throw like one? Lemme show you, now. Ya take your little crow hop like this, ya get your body behind the throw, and ya let it go. See?" With that, the fellow in his seventies who was never an out-fielder hops, digs in, and makes a perfect peg to the astonished catcher 260 feet away.

In a tryout camp of two hundred boys, there may be three or four who catch the attention of a scout, and there may not be any. Lennie has known that all along, but he can't help himself. "I'm not supposed to teach 'em," he says, gruff and sheepish at the same time, "but, ah, what the hell? Maybe I can take a kid who's on a high school team and show him a little bit about how to throw. He tries it my way, and he throws a little better. He tries it again, and he throws a little better still. He can see this happening. He can feel it. He's still not gonna be anything but a high school ballplayer, but he'll be a little better. Maybe he'll be a little happier about it."

If Lennie is a clandestine teacher of the game, he is an upfront, unapologetic baseball talker. The story about the inning of four errors is not the only one he tells at his own expense. He smiles and recalls that he wrote a scouting report on Pete Rose when Rose was in his first year of organized baseball. "New York—Penn League," Lennie recalls. "A Ball. I said there was no reason to think he'd ever play any higher. Some scout. Then, years later, Rose heard the story of that report. I think Jean [Mrs. Lennie Merullo] told him about it at some banquet we'd gone to. And, of course, he wanted the report. So, he started asking me for it, and I kept telling him no, because what do I want that thing out there for? But he and another fella, a good friend of mine who was also a friend of Pete's, they kept after me, kept calling and so on, and finally I said all right and sent him the report. Next thing I know, I get this bat in the mail from Pete Rose, and it's supposed to be the bat he used to get his first major league hit. I don't know whether it is or not, but here it is. And I've got a lot of other bats . . ."

He has a bat Ted Williams used, and one of Ty Cobb's. He's got a bat that Babe Ruth hit with, too. They have come to him from strangers who've heard him talk about baseball. Lennie Merullo is like that. People hear him and think, "There is no reason for this bat to sit in my closet. Lennie Merullo could have it. He could talk about it. He could almost make it come alive." And so, a man rummages around in the closet for the bat Ted Williams cracked slightly and flung carelessly and a little too hard toward the box seats, where the batboy would have picked it up if it hadn't hit a pebble or something and taken a crazy bounce into the lap of a surprised and delighted fan. And the next morning, even before breakfast, the son of the man who caught the bat is at Lennie Merullo's door, half embarrassed but determined. And when Lennie answers the bell, still in his pajamas, the man thrusts the bat at him and says, "You don't know me, but this is Ted Williams's bat. I thought you'd like to have it." And Lennie has another story to tell.

"This Williams bat," he says, turning it over in his shortstop's hands, "it looked so *small* to me. And Ted Williams hit all those home runs. How could he do it with a bat like this? So, they have this baseball banquet up in Manchester, New Hampshire, every winter, and one year I saw that Ted was gonna be the speaker. I put the bat in my car and took it with me when we drove up for the dinner. I was gonna show it to him and ask him if it was his. But then I got cold feet, and I left it in the car.

"So, we're sitting in the banquet hall, Jean and I and a bunch of other people at a table off to the side, and they've got us sitting next to the umpire Jim Honochick. For some reason, my wife decides she has to tell Honochick about the bat. Come to think of it, my wife has gotten me into a lot of trouble at these banquets. Anyway, all of a sudden, here's Honochick's big, meaty hand on my shoulder, and he says, 'Go get that bat.' But he doesn't just say it. He *bellows* it. *'Go get that bat!'* Jeez, half the people in the hall are lookin' over at us, wondering what's wrong. So, I got up and went out to the parking lot . . . I had to do something to quiet him down, didn't I? And when I came back in, Ted was up at the podium. I didn't want to look like an idiot, walking through the crowd to my table with a baseball bat. So I tucked it into my pants leg. But

Honochick saw me coming, and he started shouting again, 'Where the hell's the bat?'

"This time, he's got Ted Williams's attention, too, and the only way to shut Honochick up is to pull the bat out of my pants with most of the people in the room watching me. And then, of course, Ted says, 'Whata ya got there?' He's as loud as Honochick. So I hand him the bat. Ted's face lights up, and he says, 'Hey, that's one of my summer bats.' He goes on to explain how he'd start the season feeling strong, using a heavy bat. Then, as the weather would get hotter and he'd get a little tired, maybe lose a little weight, he'd switch to a lighter bat. I don't know what he'd have talked about that night if I hadn't been there, but that bat became his text for the evening. Which was fine, except that watching him heft it and half swing it up there, watching him smile at it, I was sure I'd never get it back. But I did. And now I know it's the real thing."

AT THE BALLPARK, at least, scouts have privileges. And old scouts have *more* privileges. So I am not surprised to notice Lennie Merullo in the best seat in Fenway Park an hour and a half before a game against the White Sox one night in the summer of 1989. He is behind home plate, maybe twelve rows back. Boots is with him, and Boots's son Matt would probably be there, too, except that he has just been called up by the White Sox and will be catching the game that night.

"Have you got a minute to talk?" I ask him.

"Right after batting practice," he growls. The words slide out of the side of his mouth. His eyes never leave the hitter in the cage.

Matt Merullo is a big, strong, redheaded kid. On this particular night, before family and friends, he acquits himself well. He knocks in a run with a sacrifice fly and singles hard to left center.

"You must be the proudest man in the place," I say to Lennie after the single.

"Well, I was just as proud when I watched his sister play softball for her high school team," he says. "She knocked in a *couple* of runs."

Behind the plate now, Matt Merullo takes the relief pitcher's last warm-up throw and snaps the ball down to second base as if he's been doing it in the big leagues for years.

"He *looks* as if he knows what he's doing out there," I say to Lennie.

"Yes, he does," Lennie agrees. "He looks like a ballplayer."

And Lennie himself looks as if he wishes that no one was watching him, because then he could let out the smile that would wash over the night sky of the ballpark like the sunshine of a perfect baseball day.

The Carlos Quintana look-alike pictured here, the kid with the cheeks, may or may not be hungry. Sticking the glove in one's mouth is a habit that appears to cross lines of class, culture, and gender. Somebody should probably commission a study. At least this kid isn't eating his while the game is going on. *Caracas, Venezuela.*

WINTER

BALL

PART OF THE CHARM of baseball is its apparent simplicity and its obvious order. Throw strikes. See the ball, hit the ball. Inside the line is fair, outside the line is foul.

But the relationship between baseball in the United States and *el béisbol* in Latin America is complicated to the point of mystery, a paradox raised to a power beyond imagining. The game has brought U.S.-ballplayer-style wealth to the Ozzie Guillens and Tony Peñas of the world. It has also raised against logic the hopes of thousands of others in countries where unemployment crowds 40 percent. In the Dominican Republic, which has come to be known in baseball circles as the land of a thousand middle infielders, barefoot boys with gloves made of crushed orange juice cartons play the game with grace and ferocity. They swing hard at almost everything because, as a local saying has it, "Nobody walks off the island."

But if major league baseball has enriched the very best players from Latin America, it has also to some extent impoverished *el béisbol* itself back home. Some of the newest millionaires no longer play in the Winter Leagues simply because they don't need the money. Meanwhile, the money that the big leagues pay non-Latin players has combined with the hopeless devaluation of the currency in many Latin countries to make it nearly impossible for the Winter League teams to hire top-flight gringos.

The relationship between the major league clubs and the Latin players themselves is double-edged, too. Led by the Dodgers years ago, most of the big league organizations now maintain at least skeletal scouting operations in South and Central America and in the islands. The Dodgers' camp in the Dominican Republic provides ballplayers with not only a salary, dormitory housing, and three meals a day, but with rudimentary classes in English as well. There, teenaged Dominicans learn to repeat, "It's baseball we love!" and "Baseball is our life!" in unison. Without the camps, the function of which is obviously to draw off the most worthy candidates and send them north, some of the aspiring ballplayers would no doubt be

---

In baseball, more than in any other team sport, each player is always alone. *Caracas, Venezuela.*

unemployed and hungry. But some of the others might be pursuing more likely routes out of poverty.

And then there is history. Consider that Latinos, African-Americans, and Anglos all played professional ball together on the same teams for years in Cuba, Mexico, Santo Domingo, and throughout Central and South America when they couldn't do so in the United States. Which was the undeveloped nation? Baseball came into places such as Nicaragua and Panama with the marines, the same organization that brought gunboat diplomacy, puppet governments, and protection for the sugar companies.

Now, multiply the mixed blessings and curses by Chico Carrasquel's lifetime major league batting average (.258 for Chicago, Cleveland, Kansas City, and Baltimore), and you have the complexity quotient for baseball in Venezuela. Carrasquel himself, born in Caracas, is the undisputed hero of his people, not only because he was the first Latin American to be named to a major league all-star team, and not only because he kept playing at home in the winter long after he'd made a name for himself up north in the summer. Into his sixties, Carrasquel remains a presence in Venezuelan baseball. He attends games regularly, signs autographs tirelessly, and reminisces with everybody who happens by. When you ask anyone in Venezuela why so many of the ballplayers in that country want to be shortstops, the answer is, invariably, "Chico Carrasquel." His house is an informal museum, filled with artifacts of the game, and the door is usually open. Complete strangers wander in to examine his old jerseys and inscribed baseballs.

But Carrasquel's country is alone in Latin America in not acknowledging that the origins of the game there are connected to the hemisphere's big, hungry uncle. When author John Krich (*El Béisbol*) went south in search of baseball's most far-flung frontier, he found researchers who swore that baseball in Venezuela had evolved from the British game of rounders, introduced when Englishmen were building the Venezuelan railway in the 1890s. They maintained that the Venezuelan game was essentially native, and their claim remains at least as valid as the preposterous story that U.S. baseball sprang full-blown from Abner Doubleday's imagination. In any case, let the record show (again, according to John Krich) that in 1903, when the U.S. Navy arrived to scuttle a German blockade of Venezuela's ports, the locals won the second game of a doubleheader against the Seabees to gain a split.

Whatever its origins, baseball in Venezuela is alive and popular in all sorts of manifestations. At the professional level, six teams compete for the allegiance of fans who have made "the wave" their own and augmented the noxious practice by throwing beer cups, full and empty, into the air as the

Tiberones game. *Estadio Universitario, Caracas, Venezuela.*

The bat is purple and the ball is a crushed orange juice carton, but the kid has his eye on it. Give him a contract. *Caracas, Venezuela.*

Pitchers are supposed to throw off a mound. They are supposed to wear socks. They are not supposed to wear first basemen's gloves. Tell it to the Marines. *Caracas, Venezuela.*

damn thing ripples past. Supporters of the Tigres or the Cardinales blow shrill whistles and beat on conga drums and tambourines, sometimes whipping themselves and each other into states of excitement manic enough to justify the serious police presence and patrolling guard dogs that appear on the field toward the end of the game.

Meanwhile, in the parks and in the streets, wherever construction has left space, those who have baseballs, gloves, and bats put them to use. Those who don't have the standard equipment pitch bottle caps and try to hit them with broomsticks in a game called *chapitas*. Ted Williams once said that hitting a baseball with a bat was the toughest challenge in sports, but he probably never faced a left-handed flinger of bottle caps. If he had, it would have been great practice. A real baseball would have looked as big as God's right eye. He'd probably have hit .500.

This is not to suggest that it is a good thing for children to be without real baseballs or bats. Poverty is much more often brutalizing than it is ennobling or good practice. But you can't discuss the game with old baseball men for long without hearing a lot of cranky talk regarding all the empty playgrounds in our land. The lament is that U.S. kids don't play now unless they're provided with uniforms, umpires, coaches, banquets, and trophies. This theory has it that the hungry kids are all playing basketball until midnight and beyond, while the baseball fields are left to suburban dandies who will only dabble in the game for a few seasons before casting their mitts aside to turn their attention to running the world. In Venezuela and throughout the rest of Latin America, those who mourn for stickball and pickup games that end only when it's too dark to see the ball can find their good old days. Little League is thriving south of the border, and the spiritual sons of Chico Carrasquel, Luis Tiant, Tony Perez, and the others admire themselves in their white uniforms and toss their gloves and colored caps into the air when they win.

But *chapitas* flourishes, too. Baseball adjusted to fit into narrow alleys or modified for macadam courts (where, remarkably, everybody still slides) lives in Caracas as it once did in the tenement sections of New York before basketball took over there. The standard line has it that basketball's enormous popularity in the cities is directly related to how little equipment the game requires. Everybody's got sneakers, and somebody always has a ball, so as long as nobody has vandalized the playground and stolen the rim and the backboard for scrap metal, you're all set. For baseball, you need a glove, a bat, and lots of open space, not to mention eighteen people. But that wisdom hasn't made it to Caracas—or Managua or San Pedro de Macorís. In those places, it's, "I got my broomstick. You got a bottle cap?" Play ball. And dream.

UMPIRES

HERE IS THE ONLY good reason I can think of to be an umpire: you once were a player, but you have grown too old or too slow to do that anymore, and you love the game so much that you can't bear to be out of its presence. And all the coaching jobs are filled.

Just as some people are drawn to the screech and burning rubber of the pits where racing cars jam and whine, just as some folks *must* live by the sea, some men and women feel each spring and summer the irresistible tug of baseball. For a few of them, the attraction is apparently so strong that it provokes them to become umpires.

At all levels, the abuse these people suffer is terrible. Major league umpires endure small-minded, sick little tyrants such as the late Billy Martin and bombastic clowns too numerous to mention. Many managers are wonderful family men. Often they are the best storytellers in the clubhouse. But when a call goes against them, they can turn instantly to raving, posturing bozos. They kick dirt on the umpire's shoes, spray tobacco juice in his face, and then, having been booted out of the game, they hurl bats, towels, and watercoolers in his direction for good measure.

Managers are by no means the only culprits. All good and confident hitters believe that most of the called strikes they've taken should have been called balls. Almost all pitchers who have ever given up a walk believe they were squeezed by the plate umpire. Most announcers regularly second-guess the arbiters, and some of them—Bob Starr and Joe Nuxhall, for example—openly deride them. Starr especially enjoys making fun of the ones who are overweight. And, of course, the fans practically feel obliged to hammer on the umpires. It's a responsibility that seems to come with the price of a ticket, even if admission is free.

The teenagers who volunteer to umpire kids' games and who last through a season or so probably grow up to be saints. A few years ago, in East St. Louis, a Little League father became so upset with an umpire's call that he went after the offending official with a bat. Eventually, he was restrained by the two or three responsible adults on hand, and the aggrieved

Overleaf: Here, aspiring arbiters prepare for a job where, on a good day, only one side will regard them as incompetent, dumb, and crooked. *Evaluation Course, Major League Baseball Umpire Development Program, Baseball City, FL.*

parent left the field, still screaming threats. A few innings later, he returned with a gun and got off a couple of shots in the general direction of the umpire before he was tackled and subdued again. Granted, this instance of mayhem was extreme. Most umpires at that level face nothing more ugly than ten-year-olds with braces and freckles sneering at them and calling them names. Still, for what?

And, if they do hang in there, it only gets worse. High school and college players are bigger and more menacing and sometimes as badly behaved. Only the very best coaches at those levels seem to accept the teaching of respect and self-control as part of their work, and no wonder. Only cranks believe that umpires don't deserve needling and scorn. During the last game of the American League Playoffs in 1990, Roger Clemens, baseball's most dominant pitcher at the time, became convinced that plate umpire Terry Cooney was moving the strike zone on him. After one walk too many, Clemens, whose judgment might kindly be described as minimal even in unchallenging circumstances, began baiting Cooney. When the umpire felt he'd heard enough, he tossed Clemens from the game, at which point the burly pitcher began calling him names unfit for print. The highlight of the tirade came when Clemens told Cooney that he was going to find out where he lived and "visit him" during the winter . . . a season that had already arrived for Clemens and that was only eight innings away for his teammates, thanks to their pitcher's tantrum. But the kicker to this story is that the overwhelming majority of Boston fans polled after the affair felt that the umpire had jobbed the Red Sox by failing to *warn* Roger Clemens or his manager before throwing the pitcher out of the game. Even as they watched the videotape of Clemens, blotchy with rage, out of control, doing about as much damage to his team as he could do without turning an automatic weapon on the infield, they concluded that it had all been Terry Cooney's fault. Such is the lot of the umpire.

In a fine and entertaining novel, *Conduct of the Game,* John Hough created a character who is compelled by the most laudable of motives to become an umpire. He is passionate about baseball *and* justice. He discovers early that he is comfortable representing authority; happy, even, in the role of protector of the art of baseball, which cannot exist outside of the frame established by the foul lines, the fences, and most important, the rules. Lee Malcolm, Hough's protagonist, serves a greater god than hitters who would amass three thousand hits or pitchers who would win twenty or more games. He serves baseball itself. And, for a time, the baseball gods seem to smile upon Malcolm. He makes it to the big leagues in record time. He appears to flourish. But before long the treachery of fellow umpires, the stupidity of the players, and above all, the corrupt superstructure of

Umpires have to practice, too. First in front of a mirror, then with a pitcher and a catcher, and finally with a hitter at the plate. If the ump passes at each level, they open the gates and let the crowd in. *Evaluation Course, Major League Baseball Umpire Development Program, Baseball City, FL.*

the league and the commissioner's office and the sky itself under which the game is played drive from his chosen work this good fellow who wanted only to quickly and correctly make the calls and get on with the game. Toward the end of *Conduct of the Game*, he is disillusioned and desperate enough to consider working for a newspaper instead.

John Hough's story provides a more-than-adequate blueprint for umpires who would buckle chest protectors over hearts full of ideals. Umpiring is dirty work, and nobody loves you. Bart Giamatti adored baseball more than any commissioner before him and spoke more eloquently about it than most poets could. He came from the world of academics, where such notions as truth and justice are less likely to be dismissed with a snicker than anywhere else. But even Giamatti couldn't, or wouldn't, stand up for umpires. On Giamatti's watch, Dave Pallone, a gay umpire, was drummed out of the game, and Pam Postema, who might have been the first female official in the big leagues, languished at Triple A. Under Giamatti, as during the reigns of other commissioners, umpires have been arbitrarily told to raise or lower the strike zone, call balks or not call them, check bats for cork or leave them alone, examine pitchers for nail files and sandpaper, or get on with the damn game, except when they are supposed to slow it down for television. Always, it has been the umpires who have been on the line to take the heat for these policy decisions, and always, they could be sure only that at least one side—on good days, only one side at a time—would think they were incompetent, dumb, crooked, or all three.

Okay, you say, but the professional umpires . . . the ones who work in Wrigley Field and Yankee Stadium or aspire from Wilkes-Barre, Albuquerque, or Fort Myers to do so . . . get paid. Somebody gives them money, albeit not very much, to go to work at a ballpark each day or each night. And the undeniable power of logic is at work here, because considerable evidence exists to show that many people will embrace any delusion and suffer a lot for money. But what of those who do it for free or for money too short to even park their cars for the game's duration? Go to a Municipal League fast-pitch softball game some summer night. The players will range in age from seventeen to fifty-five or so. Umpires there have been at it for thirty years sometimes. They make about fifteen dollars a game. For that, they get foul tips off the shoulders and toes and, on a bad night, the accumulated derision and rage of twenty-five or so people who've either been at work all day at jobs they hate or have no jobs at all. There, between rotted, leaning fences, while dogs and shirtless children overrun the outfield between pitches, the umpires try to keep order. The foul lines, chalked in several days ago at best, are gone by the third inning. Who

The umpire's job is to keep order in the game. His work begins with the mainte-nance of a clean, well-lighted plate. *Lake Nokomis Field, Minneapolis, MN.*

knows if a bunt is foul or fair? The kind of thick, tan dust that sticks to your teeth covers the plate constantly, and you can't sweep it after every pitch. Who knows whether that ball was really on the corner or not? In the big leagues, four umpires work a game, so even if they *feel* alone, when it comes time to make a decision, they've got more backup on hand than most cops. But if you're behind the plate in the city leagues, you're entitled to only one partner to work the bases, and if he stopped off at a bar some-where or couldn't find his way to the park because of the detour where the water main broke under the expressway, you're out of luck. It's just you and everybody who's waiting for you to screw up.

So. The most charitable interpretation of all this is perhaps that umpires are not masochists but Christians, and a case can be made. They don't so much embrace suffering and abuse as turn the other cheek. They do it as believers. The weaker among them let the managers and players and fans get under their skin. They come to see those groups as their enemies and even relish opportunities to stick it to the folks who've banged on them most mercilessly. Several former major league umpires have acknowledged that they had it in for individual nemeses. But the very best of them, whether under the big league lights or in a steady drizzle on April's coldest sandlot, simply call 'em as they see 'em and accept whatever comes next. There are, after all, worse ways to proceed.

Here is a certain bet: If and when there ever *is* a Real World Series, the Golden Rams Marching Band, or some bunch of folks very much like them, will be there. *Veterans Stadium, Philadelphia, PA.*

A REAL
WORLD SERIES

THE FIRST BASEBALL TOURNAMENT in the United States that billed itself as the World Series took place in Detroit in 1868. It was, like every "World Series" that would follow it, a fraud. It contained teams only from ten U.S. cities and three towns in Canada. Hamilton, one of the teams from Canada, won the thing.

It took fourteen years for anyone in baseball to work up sufficient brass to call another play-off in this country the World Series. By then (1882), two professional circuits, the National League and the American Association, were going strong. Or sort of strong. Chicago, of the National League, and Cincinnati, of the American Association, each won one game in the '82 series, and then for reasons that don't bear examining but that doubtless had to do with at least two different ways to count the money, the whole event fell apart amid threats and recriminations.

The annual battle between the best team in the National League and the best team in the American Association was called the World Series for another eight years, until the American Association folded. From 1894 until 1897, the first- and second-place teams in the National League finished the season by playing for the Temple Cup, a gaudy trophy vaingloriously named for William Temple, who paid for it. Temple at least had the good sense to recognize that something that involved only one league could hardly be called the World Series.

In 1903, though, the promoters were up to their old tricks again. After two seasons of debate and confusion over whether each league was sufficiently legitimate to play the other, the owners of the Pittsburgh franchise in the National League and the Boston franchise in the American League figured, "What the hell?" The best-of-nine series that followed is generally recognized as the first modern-day World Series, except by cranks and pinkos who object that baseball was already being played in lots of other places around the world, as well as by hundreds of exceptionally talented black ballplayers in many of the same cities (and sometimes the same ballparks) where the alleged "big league" clubs were operating. But who'd have paid for a ticket to something called the U.S. Baseball Championship for White Players Only? (Cap Anson, a .334 lifetime hitter for Cincinnati and a ferocious bigot, is generally discredited with keeping baseball white through that era, but he got elected to the Hall of Fame, anyway.)

Boston won the 1903 World Series, such as it was. No team in either league was housed any farther west than St. Louis, and by '03, no Canadian clubs were in the running. Still, it's fun to look up descriptions and recollections of the first modern World Serious (Ring Lardner would coin that phrase a few years later). My personal favorite comes from Freddy Parent, who played shortstop for Boston in those days. At age ninety-some, Parent said of the '03 spectacle: "I outhit Honus Wagner, and I outfielded him, too . . . but it's hard for me to remember now. You came to me too late to talk about those days, boys."

That World Series failed to establish itself as sacred and indomitable. In 1904, New York Giant manager John McGraw refused to dignify the Series with the presence of his team, claiming that the upstart American League was not worthy of his club's notice. In '05, though, McGraw relented, and then some. His Giants not only showed up, they had new uniforms made for the occasion. Then, contrary to the spirit of the grand event, several players from the Giants and from their opponents, the Philadelphia Athletics, agreed before the Series to split their shares of the purse 50-50, no matter which team won. (Some of *those* players probably got into the Hall of Fame, too.)

Since 1905, the Series has been a fixture on the American sports scene. In *One Flew Over the Cuckoo's Nest,* Ken Kesey had his main character, R. P. McMurphy, remember from his prison days that there'd have been a riot in each cell block if the warden hadn't allowed the inmates to tune in the Series on TV. But, despite the eventual presence in Major League Baseball of players from Venezuela, Cuba, the Dominican Republic, Puerto Rico, the Netherlands, Japan, and several other countries, the Serious has remained a North American event, its moniker notwithstanding. This is a shame, because baseball has gloriously outgrown the continent that contains the major leagues. It flourishes in Japan, of course, where well-established professional teams play a caliber of ball impressive enough that the success of the U.S. major leaguers who opt to play there is by no means automatic. Once, the Japanese clubs had to be content to employ fading stars who were looking to extend their paydays by a season or two when they could no longer make a major league roster. But over the past decade or so, Cecil Fielder and a number of lesser players in their primes have shuttled between Japanese and major league teams. Several of the Japanese clubs have played regularly against U.S. major league teams during the

Grapefruit and Cactus league seasons, and the teams from Japan have been competitive. In some off-seasons, when collections of U.S. all-star players have barnstormed in Japan after the major league season, teams of Japanese all-stars have won about as often as not.

Japan is not the only country that could provide a real World Series contender. The Cuban team sailed through the '92 Olympics to win the gold medal. Though the U.S. competition was a team made up of players still in college, many of those players had been chosen high in the major league draft. At least one U.S. observer was convinced the Cubans could play at a higher level. A Denver columnist, mindful of the fact that his city would be home to a major league franchise for the first time in '93, suggested that the new owners would do well to forget trying to stock the expansion Rockies by drafting players from the big league teams. He said they should simply hire the whole Cuban ball club instead.

One intriguing entry in a Real World Series would be the Dominican Republic, which has been exporting middle infielders and pitchers to the major leagues for years. Puerto Rico, Venezuela, Mexico, and several other Latin American locales are also thoroughly stocked with players who've had experience in the bigs or played winter ball against major leaguers. And, if baseball in Taiwan and the Philippines didn't essentially end with Little League (and it might not if there were a Real World Series to shoot for), the kids who've overwhelmed teams from the United States and elsewhere might grow into the next generation's Kirby Pucketts and Tom Glavines. (I know, I know, the hustlers who put together the Little League team from the Philippines cheated. But if they fielded a national team of adult players, it would be okay if they didn't all live in the same city.)

I'll grant that it wouldn't be easy to arrange the Real World Series. Organizers would have to figure out how to convince the Tony Peñas (Dominican Republic) and Dennis Martinezes (Nicaragua) and Candy Maldonados (Puerto Rico) of the world to briefly forsake the major league teams and their major league paydays in favor of service to their home countries. Maybe the best idea would be to suspend the major league season every fifth year so that foreign-born pros playing in the United States could return home and play for teams that might qualify for the Real World Series at the end of that summer. If the ensuing competition became even half as absorbing to baseball fans as the World Cup soccer tournament is to soccer fans every four years, the big leagues might not be much missed . . . a circumstance that might go some distance toward putting major leaguers into a little closer touch with reality.

I'm not quite fool enough to think that the creation of a Real World Series would carry us into Utopia or even that the members of different cultures and citizens of different countries would necessarily come to understand each other more thoroughly as a result of their participation in the thing. World Cup soccer has not brought about that result, though on some strange and wonderful days, wars *have* actually been postponed so that they wouldn't thwart the desire of soldiers on both sides to watch a soccer game. And at least the admission that the best-four-of-seven game package that concludes the baseball season in the United States and Canada each fall is *not* a "World" Series might deflate a little the smugness that characterizes the attitude of many citizens here about what goes on elsewhere on the globe.

I think, no matter where I roam,
I'll never see a handsome dome.

HHH Metrodome, Minneapolis, MN.

SUPERAMERICA

FOR IT'S 1-2-3
STRIKES YOU'RE OUT
AT THE OLD
BALL GAME

Bud
KING OF BEERS

OLD-TIMERS
AND THEIR GAMES

IN THE GOOD and bygone days of day baseball and no domes, players who came out of retirement to dress up in uniforms and play at the game for an inning or two were called old-timers. Now, they are hyped as "legends," "heroes," and "immortals," but the glorious labels fool nobody who shows up to watch. An old man is an old man, no matter who he used to be.

Still, we are at liberty to make of that fact what we will. Some delight at seeing a gray ex-pitcher toss at half speed to a paunchy ex-hitter. For some, the sight of a former outfielder bouncing and grunting to get under a fly ball he'd have caught effortlessly two decades earlier is pure entertainment. I'm told some fathers watch such goings-on and say to their sons, "He was one of the greatest, boy," and I suppose some sons are polite enough to nod, though they cannot possibly believe it.

Others would happily contribute the ticket money to the fund that helps indigent retired ballplayers and forgo the show. One sports columnist wrote recently that he wished all ex-ballplayers had as much sense as Joe DiMaggio, who always attends old-timers' games in a business suit and contents himself with nodding and waving to the fans when he is introduced, then leaving the field to others.

Fortunately for the fellows who run the baseball fantasy camps, not everybody feels the way that columnist does. Fantasy camps offer any fan willing to spend a couple thousand dollars the opportunity to dress like a ballplayer, spit like a ballplayer, and drink like a ballplayer when the game is over. Old-timers handle the instruction. There is much bantering. On the night before camp ends, dentists and investment counselors win most valuable player trophies. Business is booming, especially for the camps that cater to fans of the major league teams that have inspired especially powerful loyalties. Cubs fans who have never before met need only say, "Ernie Banks" and "Sweet Billy Williams" and "Cub Fever: Catch It . . . and Die" to one another to affirm eternal bonds. Old Red Sox fans can accomplish the same thing by mumbling, "Ted Williams," "Denny Galehouse," and "Game six."

At their best, fantasy camps generate harmless fun and sometimes a little money for charity. They give retired players the opportunity to collect a check for fooling around in the game again, and the campers come away clutching photos of their middle-aged selves with their boyhood heroes. Better late than never, perhaps, and whom does it hurt?

The camps work because so many fans carry into prosperous adulthood two goofy and childish notions: that they really *could* have been ballplayers themselves if things had broken differently and that the men who *did* become ballplayers somehow assumed an eternal glow when it happened. Many are the stories of judges, surgeons, and scholars who have visited major league dugouts and clubhouses, only to find themselves blushing and tongue-tied when faced with the opportunity to talk to some postadolescent phenom. When they return from the fantasy camps, all the players-for-a-moment can tell their golfing buddies that the ballplayers are just regular guys, and though this should not come as news to anyone, it invariably does.

The baseball fantasy camp is a natural for one other crucial reason. With a very few exceptions, active and retired baseball players are about the same size as the rest of us. The eternal glow notwithstanding, Bucky Dent, in or out of uniform, is not particularly intimidating. Willie Mays, the Giant, is two inches short of six feet. Roberto Clemente was shorter still. There are middle infielders who have to stand on milk crates to be interviewed. This fuels notion number one and lends mystery to notion number two. Fantasy campers can say, "I'm as big and strong as that guy," and then puzzle forever over the combination of genetic gifts, personality quirks, and environmental nudges and pokes that distinguish the supple, quick-wristed hitter from the studious accountant. "If my father had only played catch with me," the latter can say to himself, because there is no apparent and gross dissimilarity between himself and the ballplayers.

This perception is not limited to outsiders and wannabes. One spring, *Boston Globe* sports columnist Dan Shaughnessy was removed from the Celtics beat and assigned to the Red Sox. "Overnight I went from being old and short to young and tall," Shaughnessy said. If he was less than half serious, the fantasy campers are only a quarter or maybe an eighth kidding when they hope for the same transformation. And baseball's the only game that makes them the offer, even in fun.

At the Fantasy Camps, the luckiest dreamers pull a hamstring before they face live pitching. Everybody else goes home humble. *Red Sox Fantasy Camp, Chain O'Lakes Park, Winter Haven, FL.*

Tom Seaver and Rollie Fingers. Eventually almost everybody gets a little heavy. Everybody slows down. Everybody gets stiff. But if you're extraordinarily talented, given to hard work, lucky enough to stay healthy, and free of the compulsion to bet on baseball games, maybe you'll be in the Hall of Fame when these things happen to you. *Doubleday Field, Coopers-town, NY.*

SOME BALLPLAYERS weather better than others do.

The unlucky hang around and get cranky. They complain that they never got the money the kids are getting now and that contemporary players are paying insufficient attention to them when they decide how to distribute the pension fund. The justice of each claim is indisputable. Before Curt Flood challenged the reserve clause in 1969 and the Players' Association struck over the funding of their pensions in 1972 and gained the right to go to arbitration in salary disputes in 1973, pro ballplayers were at the mercy of their employers. Minor league ballplayers still are. But who wants to hear about this stuff? Two or three sentences on the subject have probably convinced you to turn the page, unless you're Early Wynn or Enos Slaughter.

The trick to retiring from baseball, like the trick to retiring from anything else, is to bring a little style and perhaps even grace to the occasion. Lou Gehrig, who called himself "the luckiest man on the face of the earth" though he was dying, managed that. Babe Ruth, who played too long and then deluded himself into thinking he'd be invited to manage the Yankees, did not. Willie Mays played *much* too long and utterly botched his retirement, managing at one point to get himself banished from baseball for accepting employment with an Atlantic City casino. On the other end of the spectrum is Ted Williams, who angered fans and enraged writers throughout his playing days, but who quickly ascended to sainthood when those days were gone.

Of course, it helps to be remembered as the last .400 hitter, but the Williams mystique extends well beyond the numbers, impressive as the numbers are. There are stories about virtually all ballplayers, of course. With its pauses to fill up and its cold off-season, baseball needs and cherishes stories like no other game. But Williams, who was private and public, poor and then rich, childish and selfless, flawed and heroic, is the stuff of stories as few other players have been.

He is the monstrously arrogant young man who said that he wanted to be known as the greatest hitter who had ever lived. He is also the gracious rookie who visited children in Boston hospitals and stayed in touch with them and with their families for years afterward.

He is the scientist who broke into component parts the act of hitting a baseball and talked about it with such zeal that the first time Carl Yastrzemski met him, Yaz was scared to death. He spent his first weeks in spring training trying to stay out of Williams's way, half convinced that

Ted Williams was bigger than everybody else in 1941, when he hit .406. He's still bigger than everybody else. One day, perhaps, he will die, but he will never depart our collective imagination. He will be like Elvis, but instead of showing up at the 7-11 or the Laundromat, he will materialize beside Florida batting cages to scowl at young hitters who are not swinging up. *Ted Williams, Eddie Popowski, Johnny Pesky, Eddie Pellagrini, and Bobby Doerr at Fenway Park, Boston, MA.*

Ted was crazy and utterly sure he'd never understand what the master was talking about.

Once, according to an account published nearly thirty years after Williams retired, he was walked with the bases loaded in the last half of the ninth inning to force in the winning run. He responded by throwing his bat into the air because the pitcher hadn't given him anything good to hit . . . a demonstration of seriousness of purpose and concentration on the task at hand so complete that the whole point of baseball—scoring more runs than the other team—was lost.

On another occasion, he allegedly giggled as he ran out a home run in Cleveland. The whole Cleveland team had shifted right for him, Boudreau style, and he lofted one over the left fielder's head—he was playing the equivalent of shortstop—into no-man's-land. There is no picture of Williams giggling, but at least one person from Cleveland says it happened, and if it didn't, it should have.

And then there is the oft-told tale of the only confrontation ever between Williams, the greatest of hitters, and the legendary Steve Dalkowski, the fastest pitcher who ever lived. Dalkowski never made it out of the minors, because although he averaged thirteen strikeouts per nine innings, he also averaged thirteen walks. His talent was so singular and so pure that he had no control over it. But some impresario who understood that drama is made in moments and not careers convinced Williams and Dalkowski to face each other on a spring training ball field years ago, or so the tale has it. Dalkowski threw one pitch. Williams, whose eyes were said to be so good that he could count the stitches on the ball as it came toward him, watched it unhappily, dropped his bat, and walked away. Pressed, he admitted that it was the fastest pitch he'd ever seen and that he never wanted to see it again.

You see? Look through enough Williams stories, and you will find even humility.

There are probably more stories about Ted Williams than about any other ballplayer but Babe Ruth, and in his last at bat, Williams buried even Ruth for exit lines. He hit a home run into the right-field seats at Fenway Park, and then he quit. John Updike was on hand to record the blow, which was okay because William Shakespeare and Leo Tolstoy were not available.

You could debate forever the order of the subject and his stories, like the sequence of the chicken and the egg. Is Ted Williams as real and present in baseball as he was thirty and forty and fifty years ago because the larger-than-life man accumulates stories the way the hull of a steamship accumulates barnacles? Or is it because the stories pile up on each other to create the giant?

No matter. Ted Williams carries the baggage of worship, like it or not, and in his later years, he's even found the patience to bear it. Once he would not deign to play in old-timers' games, but now he shows up and waves. He makes other public appearances. When he came to a Boston bookstore in 1987 to sign copies of an updated reissue of *The Science of Hitting*, the crowd was so large the store personnel had to shut the doors and turn off the escalator to control it. When Williams came through a side entrance, large and already rumbling, there was no cheer, just a gasp of awe. He was eleven feet tall, and when he spoke, the air cracked. Grown men wept, women fainted, and books tumbled from their shelves.

Nah. It was only Ted Williams. Only the last man to bat .400. Only the fellow who once announced that he would be the greatest hitter who ever lived, and then went out and made it happen.

Old-timers who used to be Enos Slaughter, Johnny Mize, and Ray Dandridge. *Hall of Fame Induction Ceremonies, Cooperstown, NY.*

Minor league baseball, major league vista. *Kindrick Field, home of the Helena Brewers (Pioneer League), Helena, MT.*

EPILOGUE:
CLOSING DAY

DARTMOUTH COLLEGE BASEBALL boasts association with all sorts of worthies . . . major leaguers such as Red Rolfe, Chief Meyers, and Pete Broberg, as well as a former Yale first baseman named Bush, who once missed a ground ball and went 0-for-4 at Red Rolfe Field. But big names notwithstanding, the whole idea of spring baseball in New Hampshire remains a sketchy proposition. April is hopeless there, and so is May. If it isn't raining, it's snowing. The mud is legendary. Until fairly recently, the drainage in the infield was so bad that Dartmouth had to sometimes play home games across the Lebanon line at Sachem Village. "Postponements" are common. The quotation marks are necessary because lots of the rainouts and snowouts and windchillouts are never made up. Scheduling baseball in Hanover is either an act of faith or an exercise in self-delusion, depending upon the theological underpinnings of those involved.

So when a real baseball day does manifest itself somewhere between the spring break and exams, and when a home game is actually scheduled for that day, those in attendance are likely to feel lucky to the point of giddiness. Or at least that is the way I felt early in May when I arrived in town to see Dartmouth and Holy Cross play a brisk and thoroughly satisfying nine innings. In the sunshine and good company, it was a constant effort to remind myself I was there to work.

Since I'd never been to Rolfe Field, I arrived early to gather ambience. It was everywhere. The dugouts were made of brick; pine trees stretched along the fence in left field. Somebody had wired the scratchy loudspeaker behind home plate to the radio broadcast of the Red Sox game, a bloated, untidy affair that would lumber along for three and a half hours. Dartmouth and Holy Cross would finish their business in a little less than two. There were other important distinctions. Up behind the Dartmouth dugout, a young man apparently with the college radio station was tinkering with wires and cables. He wore a T-shirt that said Dork across the back. There are a lot of dorks in any major league crowd, of course, but I've never seen one who wore the appellation for the world to see.

The game itself began badly for the home team. Rick MacDonald walked the first man he faced. A sacrifice bunt and a fly ball later, he looked as if maybe he was still worrying a little about the free pass. He'd been behind in the count early. He was throwing as if he felt he had no pitches to waste. The Holy Cross cleanup hitter jumped on a fastball that was much too good and hit it over the fence in left center and beyond the pine trees and the street as the crowd groaned or gasped. A long home run is a thing of beauty anywhere; it is a reminder, always quick and oddly surprising, no matter how often you've seen it, of how fast the tight, controlled struggle between the pitcher and the batter can disappear into the far distance. No wonder hyperbolic sportswriters sometimes call home runs "rockets" or "spaceshots." Each suddenly carries the imagination to some new place for a moment. This home run was a little too much for Rolfe Field. It ended up on a lawn between a white house and a house that will be white again someday. Mark Roman, who had hit the thing, trotted businesslike around the bases. It is one of the charms of baseball that the most admirable hitters still endeavor to look as if they have done nothing special when they turn a fastball around with their wrists and hips, changing the game utterly, bringing their own fans to their feet and reducing those on the other side to murmurs of admiration. Ted Williams never acknowledged that he'd accomplished anything much when he was running out his dingers. Neither did Mark Roman.

Pitcher MacDonald hit the next batter and walked the one after that, but before the game could sour entirely for Dartmouth, the Holy Cross first baseman popped up to end the inning.

The bottom of the first offered only a brief promise that Dartmouth might retaliate. Right fielder John Clifford, batting second, took a pitch on the hip with a thump audible across the crowded bleachers. (By this time, about two hundred fans were on hand.) A man with a sand-colored mustache and a sky-blue golf cap shouted, "Okay! We'll take it! That's a start," which is the sort of thing it's easy for fans in the soft sunshine and warm breezes to say. Nobody's throwing anything at them. That was not the only semidumb thing a fan said on that May afternoon. An inning later, a lone Dartmouth rooter standing in the shadow of the football grandstand, the steel bones of which loom huge and hideous along the entire right-field line of Rolfe as if to remind everyone which sport really matters in America, watched a Holy Cross batter offer weakly at a curveball and shouted, "Take that skirt off and swing!" The batter responded by singling hard on the next pitch. An inning later, the Holy Cross catcher dropped a perfect bunt down the first baseline and beat it out for a hit. An idiot somewhere down the bleachers screamed, "That's crap!" and the notion that Dartmouth has only knowledgeable baseball fans took another direct hit.

This is not to say that knowledge and appreciation were absent that afternoon. In the sixth, the game having settled into a fine pitchers' duel in which neither team had hit safely over four innings, I became aware of a soft but excited voice behind me. I looked over my shoulder and saw, two rows back, a fellow with two canes and a baseball cap that read, May Peace Prevail On Earth. An hour and a half earlier, I'd watched, a little puzzled, as the same man had leaned over the fence that separates the fans from the field, talking with a couple of the Dartmouth players. Now he was telling his companion stories about some of the boys . . . how this one had been hurt, but appeared to be running well now, and how that one would be trying out for the U.S. National Team. I climbed up to the seat beside this fellow, who turned out to be Stuart Griffin. He had been attending Dartmouth baseball games regularly for twelve years. He was a fan zealous enough to have traveled on the team bus to away games until the coach put a stop to it, gently explaining to Mr. Griffin that once in a while he needed a few minutes to talk to his players without anyone else in the audience.

"It's kind of funny that I've become so attached to the Dartmouth team," Mr. Griffin told me. "I went to Yale."

"Really?" I said. "What year did you graduate?"

"1939," he said.

The bleachers shifted slightly beneath me. "My father graduated from Yale in 1939," I said. "Bill Littlefield."

"Oh, sure," Mr. Griffin smiled. "I knew Bill Littlefield. He was on the crew. A good crew. They went to England one year, didn't they? To compete at Henley. And then, later on, he had a drinking problem."

"Yes," I said. "Then he stopped drinking, and he counseled alcoholics for fourteen years."

"Well, that's remarkable," he said. "He's dead now?"

"He died in 1986," I said. "In the fall."

"Well," Mr. Griffin smiled. "I remember him. He was a good golfer, too, wasn't he? And I remember many of his friends."

Poet Donald Hall once characterized baseball as "fathers playing catch with sons," which is lovely enough. But here in the bleachers was even more. Here was the memory of my father, alive and smiling before me, an oarsman, a golfer, a good man remembered. And we hadn't played catch in thirty years. When we had played, he had praised my young arm lavishly and wondered aloud why I didn't pitch. This was a lunatic notion. I had neither speed nor control. But such was the extravagant love of a non-baseball player for his only child. It was a fine memory to savor, next to my father's old classmate. So were those of weekend afternoons at the Polo Grounds with my father, watching Willie Mays and the New York Giants play, and a trip to Cooperstown, just the two of us. For a couple of days, at the age of nine or so, I wandered through the Hall of Fame, over and over, wearing my *own* Giants uniform. I wouldn't take it off. Years later, my father would delight in telling people that, on the second day, the lady at the door wouldn't take his money for my admission. He was, God bless him, too proud of his son to be embarrassed. He'd have preferred the golf course on a day like this fine one in May. But he'd have come with me if I'd asked him, and he'd have enjoyed my happiness at the ballpark.

Together, Stuart Griffin and I turned our attention back to the game. Mark Roman, the same fellow who had hit the enormous home run in the first inning, was up. On the mound, Rick MacDonald had given way to David Angeramo, but the change seemed inconsequential to the mighty Roman. He swung hard at another fastball and drove it toward deepest center field. Joe Tosone, the Dartmouth center fielder, took one look at the ball and turned his back to the infield. He ran hard for a time, snuck one peek over his left shoulder, and then reached up to pull Roman's shot out of the sky. It was as good a catch as I have ever seen at any level in any ballpark. There was the moment of silence that it always takes for people's brains to make sense of the fact that they have just seen something they couldn't have thought they would see, and then came a burst of applause and shouting.

A few minutes later, in the bottom of the eighth inning, Joe Tosone doubled sharply to left center and then scored on an error, putting Dartmouth on the board. Unfortunately for fans of the home team, that was it. The score at the end of the afternoon was 3–1, Holy Cross.

When there were two outs in the home half of the ninth, Stuart Griffin said, "It's such a beautiful day. It's a shame we can't watch more."

"It surely is," I agreed. "But I'm glad I met you. I've enjoyed talking to you. It means something to me that you knew my father and remembered him so well."

All around us now, men and women and boys and girls were rising from their seats, picking up their jackets, making plans for an early dinner or a party somewhere. There was the clatter of shoes on the metal bleachers and the bumping and scuffling of a lot of people trying to leave at once, so I wasn't sure whether Mr. Griffin had understood me, or even heard me.

Then he said, "It is so short, and so good."

So perhaps he had.

Amory Field, Brookline, MA.

Quick! Who won? *Senior Little League Championship, Medicine Hat vs. Whalley, Lethbridge, Alberta.*

ACKNOWLEDGMENTS

AMONG THE BOOKS and other works to which I've referred in writing *Baseball Days* are *The World Series, A Complete Pictorial History,* John Davaney and Burt Goldblatt, Rand McNally Press, 1972; *Baseball's Greatest Quotations,* Paul Dickson, Harper/Collins, 1991; *Cult Baseball Players,* edited by Danny Peary, Fireside Books, Simon and Schuster, 1990; *El Béisbol,* John Krich, Prentice Hall, 1989; *Once More Around the Park,* Roger Angell, Ballantine Books, 1991; *False Spring,* Pat Jordan, Dodd, Mead, 1975; *Into the Temple of Baseball,* edited by Richard Grossinger and Kevin Kerrane, Celestial Arts, 1990; *Best American Sportswriting, 1992,* edited by Glen Stout and Tom McGuane, Houghton Mifflin, 1992.

Beyond these particular books, I've learned a lot from what's been written by Peter Gammons, Dan Shaughnessy, Robert Creamer, John Hough, Thomas Boswell, and many other writers and poets by whom the game has been well served.

The second half of "Old-timers and Their Games" originally appeared in slightly different form in *Ted Williams: A Portrait in Words and Pictures,* written and edited by Glen Stout and Dick Johnson, Walker and Company, 1992.

"Pitchers and Catchers Report," "Bats," and "A Real World Series" originally aired in slightly different form on WBUR-FM in Boston or on National Public Radio's "Morning Edition," both of which I thank.

The Epilogue, "Closing Day," originally appeared in slightly different form in the *Dartmouth Alumni Magazine,* published by Dartmouth College, in the spring of 1993.

I would especially like to thank Lennie Merullo for his contagious enthusiasm, his story-telling talents, his patience, and his grin. I'd like to also thank his wife, Jean, for her warm hospitality.

Thanks also to "Morning Edition"'s Mark Schramm, a sensitive and knowledgeable editor and a wonderful companion at the ballpark, and to Tom Goldman, Mark's equally sharp and open-minded colleague. Thanks to David Greene, a great editor and even better friend.

Thanks to Jim Collins at the *Dartmouth Alumni Magazine* for commissioning "Closing Day" and for sending me Robert Kimber's *Yankee* magazine article on the R. G. Johnson Company.

Thanks to Ben "Champ" Atlee, who played away ball and remembered a lot of great stories about it.

Thanks to all the listeners who have responded to my radio work. Some have corrected me, some have suggested new ideas to consider, and many have demonstrated over and over the resilience of the love of baseball across the land.

Thanks to Curry College and the Curry College Chapter of the American Association of University Professors for agreeing on a sabbatical program that has allowed me the time to write this book.

Thanks to Jeff DiIuglio for help with Lennie Merullo's Italian and to Paula Cabral and Gabe Rice for their support at the word processor and copying machine.

Thanks to Dick Johnson for reading the manuscript of this book; to Janet Bush for editing it with grace, wisdom, and good humor; and to Patty Hansen, Christina Eckerson, and all at Bulfinch/Little, Brown.

—Bill Littlefield

I HEARTILY CONCUR with all of Bill's acknowledgments, and I'd like to add a word here for the folks who helped me make and choose the photographs.

Carlos Moreno, Patrick Harnast, and their families were the perfect hosts during my stay in Caracas. They introduced me to Juan Morales, my ideal guide (and an enthusiastic photographer), Chico Carrasquel, and so many others who helped make my time there fun and easy. Big thanks also to Catherine Harnast, who introduced me to all, and to Linda Rubuliak and Isidro Martinez, who showed me how *beisbol* is played in the barrios.

Jim Dow made a pleasant traveling companion and reliable chauffeur on two minor league jaunts. Bill Nowlin couldn't travel with me, but he shared his insights about places to go and things to capture. The same goes for Brendan Boyd and Mark Starr. Cheryl Miller, Chris Beane, Ian Tuck, and Richard Olinger assisted me at various locations. Mary Anne DiNublia transcribed my rambling notes and interviews with remarkable accuracy. And as usual, Jacquie Strasburger did far more than simply keep the home fires burning. Double ditto for Tracy Hill, my ever tolerant and multitalented assistant.

Among the many who paved the way for me in locations around the U.S.

were Bob Baird, Ralph Raymond, George Bakewell, Paul Good, Judi Kahn, Daryl Deeks, Darryl Gordon, Jack McCormick, Butch Amondsen, Ed Bradley, William Guilfoile, John Savage, Dick Bresciani, Bob Powers, Stephen Popp, and Walter Hriniak.

Lorie Novak, Ellie Hollinshead, and Fritz Drury were fair but stern photo editors. Baseball buffs Rickie Harvey and Barbara Jatkola provided the copyediting and proofreading. Doe Coover leant her considerable negotiating skills at contract time, and Mark Fischer contributed his legalese. Kaz Tsuchikawa was instrumental in distributing many of these images (and stories) in Japan. And, not least, Peter Andersen supplied the book's fine design and impeccable taste when it came time to pick the photos.

—Henry Horenstein

Frazier Field, Lynn, MA.